THE
WATCHMAN'S
WINDOW

UNLOCKING EZEKIEL'S VISIONS
IN THE LIGHT OF TODAY

DAMIANO B. CENTOLA

EXPLORA BOOKS
700 – 838 West Hastings St. Vancouver, BC V6C 0A6
www.explorabooks.com
Phone: (604) 330 6795

Bible verses are quoted from the King James Version (KJV), which is public domain, the English Standard Version (ESV), and the New King James Version (NKJV).

ISBN: 978-1-997587-88-0 *(Paperback)*
978-1-83430-029-0 *(Hardback)*
978-1-83430-030-6 *(eBook)*

THE WATCHMAN'S WINDOW

UNLOCKING EZEKIEL'S VISIONS IN THE LIGHT OF TODAY

DAMIANO B. CENTOLA

Table of Contents

Preface
The Watchman's Window:
Unlocking Ezekiel's Visions in the
Light of Today

I did not set out to write this book.

I was drawn to it—slowly, then suddenly—by the hand of God and the haunting weight of Ezekiel's visions. What began as a quiet inquiry into a single passage soon became a thunderclap in my spirit. I could not look away. I could not walk past the wheels, the fire, the bones, the river. I could not ignore the voice calling from between the cherubim, or the one crying out from the valley floor.

This book was written in that tension—between the call and the commission, between judgment and mercy, between exile and glory. Ezekiel is not an easy prophet. His visions are dense, terrifying, majestic, and often misunderstood. But they are not irrelevant.

They are not sealed. They are not finished. His writings carry the fingerprints of God's throne and the footprints of a world groaning for restoration. They pulse with urgency. They speak to leaders, to nations, to exiles, to intercessors, and to a remnant that still trembles before the Word of the Lord.

For years I studied Ezekiel in fragments—isolated moments, dramatic visions, the well-known valley of dry bones. But one day I realized: these were not scattered episodes. They were part of a divine progression, a holy architecture of revelation. The same glory that departs in Ezekiel 10 returns in Ezekiel 43. The same bones that lie dead in the valley are resurrected into an army. The same priest who was exiled becomes the prophet who sees the future temple. And between the departing and the returning, between judgment and restoration, stands a single figure: the watchman.

I believe we are living in watchman days. Days when eyes must be opened. Days when temples are desecrated and glory has lifted. Days when bones must breathe again and rivers must flow from the sanctuary of the Spirit. This is not about echoing the past. This is about discerning the present and preparing for the glory to come.

This book is for those who feel the burden.

Those who see what others cannot.

Those who have been called to warn, to weep, to watch, and to write.

This is for the exiles who still believe.

For the intercessors in the inner court.

For the sons of Zadok who know what it means to approach the altar.

If you've ever felt like Ezekiel—burdened, misunderstood, burning with a message you didn't ask for—then I invite you to walk with me through these visions, from the first fiery wheel to the final declaration:

"The Lord is There."

May the pages that follow awaken your calling, refine your vision, and stir in you the same Spirit that lifted Ezekiel between heaven and earth. May the glory return.

—Damiano B. Centola

Foreword
The Watchman's Window:
Unlocking Ezekiel's Visions in the
Light of Today
Damiano B. Centola

There are books that inform, and there are books that ignite.

This is the latter.

From the first page, The Watchman's Window opens not merely a study of Ezekiel but a portal into the burden, vision, and fire of one of Scripture's most enigmatic prophets. The Book of Ezekiel has long stood as a towering mystery—full of wheels within wheels, cryptic symbolism, and a God whose holiness is too fierce to domesticate. Many approach Ezekiel with curiosity. Few dare to inhabit it.

Damiano B. Centola is one of those few.

With the heart of a watchman and the skill of a master scribe, Centola steps into Ezekiel's world not as a distant observer but as a fellow witness—one who has felt the weight of the scroll, the ache of exile, and the hope of the returning glory. He does not treat Ezekiel as an artifact of ancient literature. He treats him as a voice that is thundering even now.

In these pages, you will not find casual theology. You will find the cry of a prophet whose voice still echoes through the smoke of judgment and the river of renewal. Centola guides us through each major vision with theological precision, spiritual clarity, and modern relevance. This is not a linear commentary. It is a spiritual excavation—uncovering the layers of meaning behind Ezekiel's visions and illuminating them for our day.

Why does this matter?

Because we are again living in days of desecrated temples and dry bones. Because we, too, have seen the glory depart. Because we are in desperate need of leaders who know what it means to stand between the porch and the altar, between heaven and earth, between warning and intercession. Ezekiel was such a man. And this book calls for more. What impressed me most is not just the insight on Ezekiel's visions, but the unwavering urgency behind every word. Centola writes like a man who has seen something—and cannot rest until others see it too. He has walked the inner courts of the temple in prayer. He has wept in the valley. He has stood on the walls with a trumpet in his hand.

This is not a book to skim. It is a book to kneel through.

My prayer is that every reader will emerge from these pages with clearer vision, deeper reverence, and renewed purpose. May the eyes of your spirit open wide. May the voice of the watchman awaken in your soul. And may the glory of the Lord once again be seen in the midst of His people.

The window is open. Look through it.

Introduction
The Eyes of the Watchman: A Prophet Between Earth and Heaven

He saw things we were not supposed to see.

He heard words that scorched the soul.

He was a man dragged by the hand of God into the whirlwind of glory and judgment.

Ezekiel — priest, prophet, exile, seer — stood between heaven and earth as the veil was torn open. The heavens opened, and the visions began. The dust of Babylon still clung to his skin, but his spirit was caught up in divine realities no eye had seen. His call was not poetic—it was painful. His scroll was not sweet—it was bitter. Yet he ate it. He watched. He warned. He wept.

This book is not just about what Ezekiel saw.

It is about what we are now seeing.

It is about the glory that left and the glory that will return.

It is about the bones, the breath, and the Bride.

It is about temples—desecrated, rebuilt, and revealed.

It is about fire, water, thresholds, and altars.

It is about Yahweh Shammah — The LORD is There.

Why Ezekiel? Why Now?

Because we live in a world where glory has departed, and few have noticed.

Because we live in a Church where idols hide behind doors, and prophets are silent.

Because the valley of dry bones stretches from nation to nation.

Because the river from the altar has begun to rise again.

Ezekiel's visions are not locked in the past. They are alive.

They are now.

They call to the watchmen, the intercessors, the repenters, the rebuilders.

This book is a window into what Ezekiel saw—but also a mirror into what we must become.

What This Book Will Do

This is not a commentary. This is not academic theology.

This is a divine decoding of vision, symbol, pattern, and Spirit.

Each chapter will walk through a portion of Ezekiel's visions—interpreting, expanding, and applying it to our generation.

- You will see the throne of God move on wheels of fire.
- You will stand in the temple and smell the burning incense.
- You will walk through the valley of bones and hear the rattling of revival.
- You will step into the river as it flows through nations and hearts.
- You will be challenged to become a watchman, a voice, a vessel.

A Word to the Remnant

If you have ever burned with the ache of God's absence...

If you have wept at the gates of compromise...

If you have longed for the weight of true glory again...

This book is for you.

You are not forgotten. You are not crazy. You are not alone.

You are a part of the Ezekiel generation—the ones who stand in Babylon but behold the Kingdom.

So, lift your eyes. Open the window.

Let Ezekiel's visions teach your spirit how to see.

Let the wind of God fill your lungs again.

Let the river of God touch your ankles. Then your knees.

Then your life.

Let the fire return to the altar of your soul.

And above all...

Let the glory return to the House.

— Damiano B. Centola

Prophetic Watchman, Scribe of Glory

Chapter 1
Wheels Within Wheels:
The Vision of the Throne

Ezekiel 1

In the thirtieth year, in the fourth month, on the fifth day of the
month, the heavens opened.

It did not begin with a voice, or a fire, or a scroll. It began
with a vision.

The prophet Ezekiel, exiled beside the river Chebar, was not looking
for glory. He was simply surviving in a foreign land, a displaced
priest with no temple, no altar, no offering. And then—without
warning or preparation—he saw it. The heavens opened, and he
looked upon a whirlwind from the north, a great cloud enfolding
itself, and a fire flashing forth continually. A brightness surrounded
it, and in the midst of the fire, something gleamed like
polished metal.

The vision that followed would shake the foundations of theology,
artistry, and cosmology itself: four living creatures, each with four
faces and four wings; wheels within wheels; eyes covering their rims;
fire darting back and forth like lightning; and above it all, the
likeness of a throne. And seated upon that throne—high above the

firmament—was the appearance of a man, glowing with fire from his waist up and from his waist down. The voice of many waters was in His presence. The glory of the Lord had not vanished.

It had moved.

The Glory That Moves

In ancient Israel, glory was tethered to geography. The Temple in Jerusalem was the dwelling place of God. The Holy of Holies was the epicenter of divine encounter. But Ezekiel's first vision shatters every preconception. God is not static. He rides in a chariot of fire, borne upon wheels, escorted by cherubim. His throne moves. His presence travels.

What Ezekiel saw was not merely artistic. It was theological. The glory of God is not bound by man's structures. It does not retire when the sanctuary is defiled. It is holy, mobile, sovereign, and uncontainable.

This revelation would be the foundation for the entire book: if the glory can depart, it can also return.

The Four Living Creatures

Each of the four living beings Ezekiel saw had four faces: the face of a man, a lion, an ox, and an eagle. Later, the Apostle John would see the same living creatures in his vision of the throne in Revelation 4. These are not fictional beasts. They are symbols of divine attributes—majesty, strength, intelligence, and speed. They are the carriers of God's glory.

They do not turn as they move. They follow the Spirit wherever He leads. Their unity is without friction. Their direction is without hesitation. They are a portrait of heavenly order, uncorrupted by human delay or rebellion.

They speak of a realm where obedience is instantaneous, where the will of God is not debated but enacted. These creatures are not only guardians; they are mirrors. They reflect the nature of the One who sits upon the throne.

Wheels Full of Eyes

The wheels within wheels remain one of the most mysterious images in all of Scripture. They moved in four directions, without turning. Their rims were full of eyes. They were vast, radiant, and living. These were not inanimate mechanisms. They were spiritual instruments, able to perceive, respond, and reveal.

The eyes speak of omniscience. The movement speaks of omnipresence. The interconnectedness of the wheels speaks of divine orchestration—where nothing happens apart from heavenly alignment. Every motion in heaven impacts the earth. Nothing is random. The wheels are turning even when men think God is silent.

For Ezekiel, the wheels would become a theological cornerstone: if God's throne has wheels, then exile is not the end. Even in Babylon, the heavens can open. Even in judgment, the throne is moving.

Above the Firmament

The vision crescendos with the sight of a sapphire throne above a crystal expanse. And upon it—the appearance of a man. Fiery, glorious, radiant. This is the pre-incarnate Christ, the Son of Man before Bethlehem. Ezekiel saw Him as Daniel saw Him, as John would later see Him: full of fire, encircled by a rainbow of glory, seated in sovereignty.

This throne was not empty. It was not metaphorical. It was not a mirage. God reigns—even in exile. His voice thunders from the heights. His presence hovers above the chaos. His likeness is wrapped in radiance.

The chapter closes with the only appropriate response: Ezekiel falls on his face.

When theology becomes vision, and vision becomes reality, there is only one posture: worship.

Why This Vision Still Speaks

In our generation, we have built pulpits but lost sight of the throne. We have constructed altars but neglected the fire. We have quoted Scripture but forgotten the eyes that search the earth. Ezekiel's vision returns us to the center: God is enthroned, alive, watching, and moving.

This chapter is not ancient poetry. It is prophetic architecture. It reintroduces the majesty of God to a world too familiar with comfort and too unfamiliar with awe.

For the modern Church, the message is clear:

We must return to the throne.

We must see again the wheels within wheels.

We must recover the fear of the Lord.

We must remember the fire.

Because only those who see the glory rightly are qualified to carry the message faithfully.

Chapter 2
Called to Eat the Scroll — A
Prophet's Burden and Boldness

Ezekiel 2–3

When Ezekiel saw the glory, he fell.

When he heard the voice, he stood.

When he received the scroll, he ate.

This was not a calling of comfort. It was a calling of fire.

The vision had barely settled when the voice of God began to speak.

"Son of man, stand upon your feet, and I will speak to thee." With

these words, Ezekiel was summoned into divine commission—not

by his own strength, but by the Spirit entering him and setting him

upright. The calling of a prophet does not begin with human

initiative. It begins with the invasion of God's presence.

The Call in Exile

Ezekiel was a priest by lineage, but a prophet by divine interruption.

His calling came not in Jerusalem, not in the temple, but in the land

of captivity. Babylon became the backdrop for the beginning of his

ministry.

This alone is a profound message: God does not need comfort

zones to speak. He calls prophets in places of judgment. He

commissions them where everything seems lost. Ezekiel's call came not in a palace but beside a polluted river. Yet from that place of exile, a voice thundered.

"Son of man, I send thee to the children of Israel, to a rebellious nation… they are impudent children and stiff-hearted."

The assignment was clear. The audience was resistant. The mission would not be easy.

God did not soften the truth. He did not promise applause. He did not cloak the message in pleasantries. He told Ezekiel the truth: they will not listen. They are rebellious. But whether they hear or forbear, they will know that a prophet has been among them.

This is the sacred paradox of prophetic ministry: the results do not validate the assignment. Obedience does.

Eat This Scroll

Then came the scroll—written on both sides, filled with lamentation, mourning, and woe. God did not ask Ezekiel to read it. He asked him to eat it.

Prophets do not merely proclaim messages. They embody them. To eat the scroll is to internalize the Word until it becomes inseparable from your bones. It is not sermon material. It is soul formation. The scroll was not sweet in content—but in obedience, it became sweet as honey in the mouth. The weight of divine sorrow became a source of intimacy. The pain of the Word became the joy of the assignment.

Only those who have eaten the scroll can speak with the authority of heaven.

A Forehead Like Flint

God then told Ezekiel something astonishing: "Behold, I have made thy face strong against their faces, and thy forehead strong against their foreheads… as an adamant harder than flint have I made thy forehead."

This was not encouragement. It was fortification.

Ezekiel was being formed into a vessel that could withstand resistance. The prophetic office is not for the faint of heart. It requires a backbone forged in prayer, a forehead set like stone, and a heart broken in secret. To be prophetic is not to be popular. It is to be unshakable.

God promised Ezekiel something better than success—He promised him presence: "Fear them not… I am with thee."

This was the same promise given to Moses, to Jeremiah, to Paul, and to every servant who would carry the fire of divine truth: You will not be alone.

Seven Days of Silence

After receiving the scroll and the commission, Ezekiel was lifted by the Spirit and taken to the exiles by the river Chebar. He sat among them—astonished—for seven days.

Seven days of silence. Seven days of observation. Seven days to absorb the gravity of the call.

In Jewish tradition, sitting seven days in silence is associated with mourning. Ezekiel was not simply stunned. He was grieving. He had seen the glory. He had heard the judgment. He now sat in the midst of a people unaware that destruction loomed.

True prophetic ministry requires a season of silence before it speaks. There must be grief before there is fire. There must be tears before there is thunder. The prophet must weep before he declares

The Watchman Anointed

At the end of those seven days, the Lord spoke again: "Son of man, I have made thee a watchman."

The watchman is not a casual observer. He is stationed on the wall, alert to the signs of danger, assigned to warn the city. If he sounds the alarm and the people ignore it, their blood is on their own hands. But if he fails to warn them, their blood is on his.

This was not poetic language. It was legal. Moral. Eternal.

God was placing Ezekiel under divine accountability: to remain silent in the face of judgment was not only failure—it was bloodguilt.

Today, many crave the title of prophet, but few understand the cost. The watchman is not defined by insight alone, but by faithfulness to declare what is seen. Silence becomes sin when it replaces obedience.

Our Generation's Scroll

In this generation, there are many words, many voices, many platforms—but few who have eaten the scroll. Few who have been stunned into silence. Few who fear the blood of others on their hands.

Ezekiel's call is not a relic of the past. It is a template for every prophetic soul today.

Have you seen enough to be burdened?

Have you eaten enough to be changed?

Have you wept enough to be entrusted with fire?

Then you are ready.

Stand on your feet.

Open your mouth.

Sound the alarm.

Whether they listen or not, let them know: a prophet has walked among them.

Damiano B. Centola

Chapter 3
The Watchman Appointed —
Warning, Blood, and
Responsibility

Ezekiel 3:16–27

The silence ended with a word of accountability.

After seven days of sitting in stunned stillness among the exiles,
Ezekiel heard the voice of the Lord again. This time, it was not a
vision. It was a charge.

"Son of man, I have made thee a watchman unto the house of
Israel: therefore hear the word at My mouth, and give them warning
from Me."

With that sentence, Ezekiel's role shifted from recipient of
revelation to bearer of responsibility. He was no longer only the one
who saw—he was now the one who must speak.

The vision had prepared him. The scroll had changed him. Now the
appointment would define him.

The Watchman's Role

In ancient cities, watchmen stood on the walls—elevated, alert, and
entrusted. Their task was not entertainment, commentary, or
personal reflection. Their task was to warn. They looked into the

distance, scanning for signs of danger, and when they saw the approach of enemies, they lifted their voices and sounded the trumpet.

The spiritual watchman is no different.

God appoints prophets not merely to reveal, but to warn. Not to soothe the crowd, but to shake the walls. Not to flatter, but to awaken. The urgency of this role is embedded in the language God uses with Ezekiel—life and death hang in the balance. If the watchman warns and the people ignore it, the guilt is theirs. But if the watchman remains silent, their blood is required at his hand. This is not metaphor. It is divine indictment. Silence, when God has spoken, is not humility—it is sin.

Four Scenarios of Accountability

God outlines four scenarios to make the point unmistakable:

- The Wicked Man Warned and Unrepentant:: If the wicked is warned but does not turn, he will die in his iniquity. The watchman is innocent.
- The Wicked Man Unwarned and Perishes: If the watchman fails to warn, the man dies, and the prophet is held responsible.
- The Righteous Man Warned and Preserved: If the righteous man is turning toward sin and is warned, and he listens, his soul is saved.
- The Righteous Man Unwarned and Falls: If the watchman fails to speak and the righteous turns to sin and perishes, the prophet bears the guilt.

This is the moral architecture of prophetic ministry. The standard is not applause or acceptance. It is obedience to the assignment and faithfulness to the warning.

Ezekiel was not commissioned to convert the people. He was commissioned to confront them.

The Weight of Blood

The phrase "his blood will I require at your hand" is among the most sobering in all of Scripture. It is not symbolic. It echoes the seriousness with which God views spiritual responsibility. The watchman does not speak for himself. He speaks for God. And what is ignored may condemn the hearer—but what is withheld may condemn the prophet.

This is the terror and glory of ministry. It is the reason Paul, centuries later, could say to the Ephesian elders, "I am pure from the blood of all men, for I have not shunned to declare unto you all the counsel of God" (Acts 20:26–27). Paul understood the Ezekiel paradigm. Silence is never neutral.

The calling is not simply to have the truth, but to declare it fully, regardless of outcome.

Muzzled by God

Following this commissioning, something unexpected happens. God tells Ezekiel that he will be made mute. His mouth will be shut—unable to speak to the people—unless and until the word of the Lord comes.

"I will make thy tongue cleave to the roof of thy mouth, that thou shalt be dumb, and shalt not be to them a reprover: for they are a rebellious house."

This silence was not punishment. It was consecration.

Ezekiel would not be allowed to speak from his own opinion, from human frustration, or out of personal reaction. He would only speak when God opened his mouth. His voice was not his own. It belonged to heaven.

In a generation of endless commentary and noise, this detail is profound: the prophetic voice is most trusted when it is most restrained.

When God did open Ezekiel's mouth, the words carried fire. But when God withheld the word, Ezekiel remained silent, even when the people rebelled. This is what made him credible. He had no agenda but obedience. He did not perform. He did not posture. He waited until the Word came.

This silence trained him. It also judged the people.

They had hardened their hearts so thoroughly that God would allow them to sit in their rebellion—unwarned—until the appointed time. The silence of the prophet became part of the judgment.

There is a time to speak. And there is a time to be withheld. The prophet must discern the difference.

The Modern Watchman

Today's watchmen are no longer stationed on stone walls, but they are still called.

They are called to see what is coming—spiritually, morally, culturally. They are called to warn the body of Christ, to cry out against sin, to proclaim the holiness of God. But they are also called to speak only when God commands. Not when pressured. Not when provoked. Not when it is convenient.

They must eat the scroll. They must sit in silence. And they must be willing to sound the alarm, even when no one listens.

God is still watching the watchmen.

The question is not whether judgment is approaching—it is. The question is whether the watchmen will cry out.

Chapter 4
Abominations in the Temple —
When Leaders Hide
Their Sin

Ezekiel 8

It began with a vision, then a scroll, then a charge.

But now Ezekiel would be shown the reason for judgment.

The cause of glory's departure was not in the heavens.

It was in the temple.

In the sixth year, in the sixth month, on the fifth day of the month, the hand of the Lord fell upon Ezekiel where he sat in his house. The elders of Judah were before him, unaware of the divine interruption about to occur. Suddenly, the prophet was caught up by a vision once again—lifted by the Spirit between earth and heaven and brought to the very threshold of the temple in Jerusalem. There, through the eyes of God, Ezekiel would witness the unseen corruption of Israel's spiritual leadership.

The sin was not in the streets.

It was in the sanctuary.

The Image of Jealousy

The first scene Ezekiel was shown was the "image of jealousy"—an idol that provoked the Lord to wrath—standing at the entrance of the temple gate. This abomination had been placed directly in the place where the presence of God once dwelt. It was not a forgotten idol tucked in the outer courts. It was deliberately installed in the inner places of worship. It was an open act of defiance. An idol in the sanctuary was not simply rebellion. It was replacement.

And yet, the glory of God was still there—at least for a moment. Ezekiel writes, "Behold, the glory of the God of Israel was there, according to the vision that I saw in the plain" (Ezekiel 8:4). The Lord had not yet departed, but He was being provoked. He was revealing to Ezekiel the reason why His presence would soon lift. The first sin was public idolatry. But what followed was more disturbing: the hidden sins of the elders.

Dig Through the Wall

God then told Ezekiel, "Son of man, dig now in the wall." So, the prophet dug. What he found was a door—hidden, obscured, concealed. And behind that door was a room full of engraved images—creeping things, abominable beasts, idols carved on every wall. Seventy elders of Israel were there, each with a censer in his hand, offering incense in secret.

Then came the chilling line:

> *"For they say, The Lord seeth us not; the Lord hath forsaken the earth."*

These were the leaders of the nation. Men entrusted with spiritual guidance. And yet they were engaged in secret idolatry—images on the wall, rituals in the dark, hidden chambers of corruption within the temple itself.

They had built a secret theology to justify their compromise: God no longer sees. He has forsaken us. We are free to do what we please.

This is the deadliest form of apostasy—not open rebellion, but hidden compromise masked by sacred garments. Not the denial of God's existence, but the denial of His presence.

They still burned incense. They still played the part. But behind closed doors, they bowed to other gods.

Ezekiel was not being shown pagan practices in foreign lands. He was being shown the secret life of Israel's elders.

The judgment that was coming to Israel was not unjust. It was inevitable. The temple had become a house of lies.

Women Weeping for Tammuz

As if this were not enough, God took Ezekiel to another part of the temple. There, he saw women weeping for Tammuz—a Mesopotamian fertility god, associated with seasonal death and rebirth. The ritual involved sensual mourning, symbolic lamentation, and pagan identification.

This was not emotional sorrow. It was spiritual betrayal.

The people of God had absorbed the rituals of their captors and integrated them into the temple's rhythm. The mourning of the daughters of Zion was no longer directed toward Yahweh—it was directed toward false gods, myths, and seductive emotions.

They were moved, but not repentant.

They wept, but not for holiness.

Today, many worship experiences are filled with emotional energy but void of reverence. Tears do not always indicate truth. Sorrow is not always repentance. The women weeping for Tammuz were sincere—but sincerely deceived.

When passion is not tethered to truth, it becomes manipulation.

When emotion replaces Scripture, idolatry is not far behind.

Turning Their Backs to the Temple

The final abomination Ezekiel saw was this: twenty-five men standing between the porch and the altar, facing east—with their backs to the temple of the Lord—worshiping the sun.

These were priests and spiritual officials, performing public worship in full view of the sanctuary. But instead of facing the Holy of Holies, they had turned their backs on it. Instead of lifting their hands toward the ark of the covenant, they stretched them toward the rising sun.

The symbolism is devastating.

They had literally and spiritually turned their backs on God.

The place of prayer had become a platform for paganism. The priests were using their authority to direct worship away from the presence of the Lord.

This was the climax of desecration.

When leaders no longer tremble in the presence of God—when they no longer face the altar, no longer guard the inner court, no longer value the glory—they become instruments of idolatry.

And the result is judgment.

The Sin Behind the Door

Ezekiel 8 is not just a chapter of history. It is a mirror.

It is a revelation of what happens when those entrusted with sacred things begin to treat them as common.

Today, we still have "images of jealousy"—ideologies that provoke the Lord.

We still have "secret chambers"—places where leaders hide compromise behind charisma.

We still have "emotional rituals"—forms of worship that stir the flesh but starve the spirit.

We still have "backs turned to the temple"—ministries that use the name of God to promote self.

The question is not whether Ezekiel's vision still speaks.

The question is whether we will let it pierce us.

The glory does not leave randomly.

It departs when the house is defiled.

But the good news is this: the vision did not end here.

There is still a remnant.

There is still a scroll.

There is still a river.

There is still a return.

But first, the abominations must be exposed.

Chapter 5
Marking the Foreheads — Divine Protection and Judgment

Ezekiel 9

The vision now intensifies.

The abominations in the temple have been exposed. The secret sins of the elders, the false mourning of the women, the priests who turned their backs on the presence of God—Ezekiel has seen it all.

But now, the Lord responds.

The judgment does not begin in Babylon.

It does not begin in the nations.

It begins in the house of God.

"Cause them that have charge over the city to draw near, every man with his destroying weapon in his hand."

What Ezekiel sees next is terrifying.

Six men approach, each with a slaughter weapon. But among them is a seventh—a man clothed in linen, with a writer's inkhorn at his side. This man does not come to destroy. He comes to mark.

God commands him to go through the midst of the city and set a mark upon the foreheads of the men that sigh and cry over all the abominations committed within it.

This is the dividing line.

This is the remnant.

This is how God separates those who merely observe from those who grieve.

The Mark of the Mourners

The Hebrew word used for "mark" in Ezekiel 9:4 is tav—the last letter of the Hebrew alphabet, shaped in ancient script like a cross. It is not simply a symbol. It is a sign of divine ownership. A seal of preservation. A visible declaration that this soul belongs to God. But not all were marked. Only those who sighed and cried—those who felt the weight of the nation's sin and grieved it. Not those who ignored it. Not those who enabled it. Not even those who recognized it—but those who wept over it.

The protection of God was not reserved for the powerful or the influential, but for the brokenhearted.

The true remnant is always found among the mourners.

They are not loud. They are not popular. But their tears move heaven.

Judgment Begins at the Sanctuary

Once the man in linen goes forth to seal the righteous, the six others are commanded to begin the judgment—at the sanctuary. God says, "Begin at My sanctuary." And they begin with the elders who stood before the house.

This order is not arbitrary. It is revelatory.

Those who are entrusted with spiritual leadership bear the greatest accountability. The judgment begins with the priests, not the pagans.

With the elders, not the outsiders. With the inner court, not the outer world.

The Apostle Peter would later echo this sobering truth:

> *"For the time is come that judgment must begin at the house of God" (1 Peter 4:17)*

If the sanctuary is corrupt, the whole nation is vulnerable.

If the altar is polluted, no offering can be accepted.

If the leaders fall, the people stagger.

God is not unjust. He begins where the truth was first revealed— where responsibility was highest and light was most accessible.

Ezekiel watches in horror as the vision unfolds. The slayers move through the city, sparing none except those who bear the mark.

Men, women, children. The judgment is absolute.

And yet one figure remains untouched: the man in linen.

He has one assignment—to seal the intercessors.

The Intercessor's Cry

As the vision unfolds, Ezekiel breaks. He falls on his face and cries out: "Ah Lord God! Wilt thou destroy all the residue of Israel in thy pouring out of fury upon Jerusalem?"

This is the heart of the true prophet.

He does not delight in judgment.

He pleads for mercy even when judgment is just.

Ezekiel's cry echoes Moses, who interceded for Israel after the golden calf. It echoes Daniel, who confessed the sins of the nation from exile. It echoes Jeremiah, who wept over Jerusalem's fall. And it echoes Jesus, who wept over the city that rejected Him.

True prophetic vision leads to intercession, not condemnation.

The watchman does not gloat. He groans.

In response to Ezekiel's plea, the Lord simply declares the reality:

"The iniquity of the house of Israel and Judah is
exceeding great... and as for Me also, Mine eye shall
not spare."

The judgment must proceed. But it will not consume the marked.

The Man in Linen Returns

Finally, the man clothed in linen returns to give his report: "I have done as Thou hast commanded me."

The statement is brief, but profound.

The mission of mercy was successful. The mourners have been sealed. The intercessors have been claimed. The sighing ones are now set apart.

He does not need to justify or explain. He simply obeys.

The mark is in place. The judgment has begun. The distinction is now clear.

The Theology of the Mark

This moment in Ezekiel's vision mirrors other moments in redemptive history:

- In Exodus, the blood of the lamb was applied to the doorposts.
- In Revelation, the 144,000 are sealed on their foreheads.
- In Romans, the Spirit bears witness that we are the children of God.

God always knows who belongs to Him.

And He always makes provision to preserve the remnant.

But the mark is never given to the apathetic.

It is reserved for the sighers and criers—those who feel what God feels and carry His burden.

In a generation that is numb, distracted, and entertained, this truth cuts deeply:

God is still marking those who mourn.

He is still separating those who intercede.

He is still sparing those who sigh.

The invitation is not to perform.

It is to grieve.

To kneel.

To be marked.

Chapter 6
The Glory Leaves the House —
Ichabod Over the City

Ezekiel 10–11

It is the moment no prophet ever wishes to see.

The point where the patience of God meets the pollution of the sanctuary.

The moment when the presence that once filled the house begins to rise and withdraw.

Ezekiel's vision continues—not with fire and thunder, but with a departure.

The glory of God is leaving.

This is not metaphor. It is not spiritual drift. It is a literal, visible movement of the manifest presence of God—lifting, pausing, hesitating, and finally withdrawing from the place He once called home.

What began as a garden in Eden became a tabernacle in the wilderness, then a temple in Jerusalem. At each stage, God dwelled among His people—not as an idea, but in fire, in cloud, in glory. But now, in Ezekiel's lifetime, that presence is preparing to depart.

The Cherubim and the Wheels

Ezekiel is once again transported by the Spirit to the threshold of the temple. There, he sees the same four cherubim he first beheld in chapter one—each with four faces, wings that touched, and wheels beside them filled with eyes.

These are not mere symbols. They are the throne-bearers of God. They move only as the Spirit moves. They are the guardians of divine order and heavenly judgment.

The man in linen, the same one who marked the intercessors in chapter nine, is now commanded to go in among the wheels and take coals of fire from between the cherubim. He is to scatter them over the city.

This act is not ritual. It is judgment.

The fire that once burned on the altar for atonement is now the fire that will fall in wrath. Jerusalem, like Sodom before her, will feel the weight of holy fire—not because God is cruel, but because the people have defiled the place of mercy.

When the altar is mocked, fire will still fall—but it will not purify. It will consume.

The Stages of Departure

Ezekiel witnesses a terrifying, gradual withdrawal of the glory:

1. First, the glory moves from between the cherubim to the threshold of the temple (Ezekiel 10:4). The house is filled with the cloud, and the court is full of brightness. God is still present—but He is no longer enthroned in the Holy of Holies. He has risen. He is pausing.
2. Then, the glory moves to the eastern gate of the Lord's house (Ezekiel 10:18–19). This is no longer hesitation. It is preparation to depart. The cherubim and wheels accompany

Him, signaling that the divine presence is leaving with order and purpose.
3. Finally, in Ezekiel 11:23, the glory of the Lord ascends from the midst of the city and stands upon the mountain east of Jerusalem—the Mount of Olives.

The presence has left the temple.

It has left the city.

It now hovers outside, watching.

This is the biblical definition of Ichabod— "The glory has departed."

And it does not depart instantly.

It lifts in stages.

As if waiting—one final chance—one final opportunity for repentance.

But none comes.

And so, the presence goes.

The Silent Judgment of Departure

There is no plague, no thunder, no announcement from heaven.

No trumpet blast. No fiery voice.

Just a lifting.

This is the most terrifying form of judgment: when God quietly departs.

No temple official notices. No priest objects. No intercessor intervenes.

The routines continue. The rituals go on.

But the presence is gone.

This is the danger of religious machinery: it can keep functioning long after God has left the building.

Ichabod does not always announce itself with collapse. Sometimes, it looks like business as usual.

But heaven is empty.

The throne is mobile.

The glory is gone.

The Heart of God in Judgment

Even in this departure, God speaks through Ezekiel. Before the final ascension of the glory, the Lord declares His anguish:

> *"I will scatter them among the countries, yet will I be*
>
> *to them as a little sanctuary in the countries where*
>
> *they shall come."*
>
> *—Ezekiel 11:16*

Though judgment has come, mercy is not absent.

Though the temple is forsaken, the people are not forgotten.

God promises that He Himself will become a sanctuary to the remnant.

Not a building. Not a system. But His own presence—wherever they go.

This is grace in exile.

A whisper of covenant amid catastrophe.

And then, the promise:

> *"I will give them one heart, and I will put a new spirit*
>
> *within you... And they shall be My people, and I will be*
>
> *their God."*
>
> *—Ezekiel 11:19–20*

Even as He departs, He prophesies return.

The glory leaves the temple, but not forever.

It will return—but only when the hearts of the people are ready.

The Glory on the Mount of Olives

The last place the glory is seen is on the Mount of Olives.

This is not incidental.

Centuries later, another Prophet would ascend from that very mountain.

One who wept over Jerusalem.

One who overturned temple tables.

One who declared, "Your house is left unto you desolate."

Jesus, the embodiment of glory, would stand on that same mount and promise His return.

The glory did not abandon Israel.

It waited for its fulfillment.

And it will return again.

When Glory Departs

Today, many houses of worship still bear the name of God.

But is the glory present?

Has the cloud lifted while the programs remain?

Has the fire been replaced by form?

Has the Spirit moved, while the leaders stayed?

Ezekiel 10 and 11 are not just historical accounts. They are warnings.

God's presence is not to be presumed upon.

His holiness is not ornamental.

When His sanctuary is profaned, He will rise.

But He also leaves a promise:

> *"I will return when the hearts return. I will dwell*
> *again when the people tremble again. I will come in*
> *glory when you prepare the house."*

This is not the end of the story.

But it is the end of an era.

The vision fades.

The glory stands on the mountain.

The city sleeps.

The prophet weeps.

And the watchman watches.

Chapter 7
The Parables of Rebellion —
Clay, Vine, and Lions

Ezekiel 12–19

With the glory now lifted and judgment looming, God begins to speak in riddles.

No longer does He thunder from the firmament or shine from the threshold.

He speaks instead in signs, actions, parables, and metaphors—

Not because He is obscure,

but because the people have become deaf.

They will not hear truth plainly.

So, He paints it in symbols.

He puts judgment into pictures.

And He turns the prophet into the message.

Ezekiel becomes not only the voice of God, but the living parable of divine grief.

Each image carries weight.

Each act is a sermon.

Each metaphor is mercy—one final attempt to awaken hardened hearts.

Signs to a Rebellious House

In Ezekiel 12, God commands the prophet to pack his belongings by day and dig through a wall by night—a sign of exile and captivity. He is to act as though he is fleeing, with his face covered, unable to see the land. When the people ask why, Ezekiel is to say:

"I am your sign."

This is the role of the prophet: not only to speak truth, but to embody it.

God turns Ezekiel into a visible warning—a walking sermon of coming judgment.

The people had said, "The vision is for many days to come."

But God replies, "There shall none of My words be prolonged anymore."

Judgment is no longer distant. It is near.

The drama is unfolding in real time.

The Parable of the Useless Vine

In chapter 15, God speaks again—this time through the image of a vine.

"What is the vine tree more than any tree?" He asks.

A vine is not used for building. It is not carved into furniture.

Its only value is in bearing fruit.

If it bears no fruit, it is fuel for the fire.

This is a piercing indictment against Jerusalem.

The city was chosen, planted, nourished by God—but it bore no fruit.

It had no strength, no honor, no yield.

And now, it would be thrown into the fire.

Jesus would echo this same warning centuries later:

"I am the true vine... every branch in Me that beareth

not fruit, He taketh away"

—John 15:1–2

Fruitlessness is not neutral.

It invites fire.

This parable reminds us: the people of God are not preserved by name alone.

Covenant requires response.

And where there is no fruit, judgment comes.

The Parable of the Adulterous Bride

Chapter 16 is one of the most graphic, heartbreaking chapters in all of prophetic literature.

It is not a riddle—it is a divine lament.

God recounts Israel's history through the image of a forsaken infant, left to die, still wallowing in blood.

But He came, saw her, and said, "Live."

He covered her. He raised her. He adorned her as a bride.

She became beautiful because of His love.

But then—she forgot.

She trusted in her beauty and played the harlot with every nation that passed by.

She offered herself to idols.

She sacrificed her children.

She traded intimacy for false promises.

And she became worse than Sodom.

God's grief is almost unbearable in this chapter.

He is not distant.

He is betrayed.

He says, "I spread My skirt over thee… and thou didst trust in thine own beauty."

This is not legal language.

It is covenantal sorrow.

And yet, at the end of the indictment comes a whisper of mercy:

> *"Nevertheless, I will remember My covenant with thee*
> *in the days of thy youth… and I will establish unto thee*
> *an everlasting covenant."*

Even the adulterous bride is not abandoned forever.

The fire of judgment will come.

But so will the refining flame of mercy.

The Parable of the Two Eagles and the Vine

In chapter 17, God speaks of two great eagles—symbols of Babylon and Egypt—who interact with a vine. The parable tells of Israel's misplaced alliances, its desire for protection outside the will of God, and its failure to remain planted where the Lord had placed it.

The message is simple:

Do not look to foreign powers to save you from the discipline of God.

Israel sought treaties and escape instead of repentance.

She turned to Egypt for security, while ignoring the covenant.

But God says, "Shall it prosper? Shall it not utterly wither when the east wind toucheth it?"

Every alliance built outside of obedience will wither.

But once again, the chapter ends with a seed of hope:

> *"I will also take of the highest branch of the high*
> *cedar... and will plant it in a high mountain... and it*
> *shall bring forth boughs, and bear fruit."*

Though Israel will fall, God will raise up a new shoot—a foreshadowing of the Messianic Branch, planted by the Lord, fruitful and strong.

The Parable of the Two Sisters: Oholah and Oholibah

Chapter 23 reintroduces the same imagery with even greater intensity.

Two sisters—Oholah (Samaria) and Oholibah (Jerusalem)—are depicted as women who prostituted themselves with the nations around them. They lusted after foreign lovers, engaged in abominations, and defiled their own sanctuaries.

This is not just immorality. It is spiritual adultery.

God recounts their actions not as distant judgment but with language that reveals heartbreak, betrayal, and holy anger.

This passage is difficult to read. It is graphic, unfiltered, and raw.

But it shows us the cost of covenant unfaithfulness.

God is not indifferent to betrayal. He is wounded by it.

Yet even here, He longs for restoration.

Why Parables?

Why does God speak in riddles, signs, and stories?

Because the people would no longer listen to direct commands.

They needed to see it. To act it out. To be forced to interpret their own reflection.

Parables pierce where arguments fail.

They bypass pride and unsettle the heart.

They force a confrontation with the soul.

This is the mercy of metaphor: it invites repentance before the sword falls.

The Prophetic Task of Interpretation

Today, we live again in a world of parables—acted out in culture, politics, pulpits, and homes.

- The clay is being reshaped by foreign hands.
- The vine is drying up on walls of compromise.
- The lions are devouring their young.
- The harlot still sits at the gate, promising pleasure and delivering chains.

And still, the Spirit asks:

Who will interpret the parable?

Who will live the sign?

Who will grieve over the meaning?

Ezekiel did not only speak the vision—he became it.

And the same call echoes now.

Chapter 8
The False Prophets and the
Wall of Lies

Ezekiel 13

They wore the robes.

They carried the language.

They claimed the mantle of the Lord.

But their visions were empty.

Their promises were false.

Their words were not from heaven.

Ezekiel 13 is a divine indictment—not against pagans or outsiders,
but against false prophets who prophesied from their own hearts.
God commands Ezekiel to speak against them, to expose their
deception, and to declare judgment upon the prophets of Israel who
claimed divine authority without divine origin.

This is one of the clearest chapters in all of Scripture on what
happens when spiritual leadership is driven by ambition instead of
obedience, imagination instead of revelation, comfort instead of
truth.

"Woe to the Foolish Prophets"

The chapter opens with a thunderous rebuke:

"Woe unto the foolish prophets, that follow their own

spirit, and have seen nothing!"

Ezekiel 13:3

These were not prophets in name only. They were active. Visible. Speaking often.

But God declares they have seen nothing.

Their visions were not from the throne.

Their dreams were not from the Spirit.

Their proclamations were not rooted in truth.

They followed their own spirit—and then claimed it was God.

This is the definition of false prophecy:

A man speaks his own words and stamps the name of the Lord upon them.

In doing so, he deceives others, exalts himself, and misrepresents the character of God.

Building the Wall with Untempered Mortar

God then gives Ezekiel a striking metaphor:

These prophets are like builders who erect a wall, but plaster it with untempered mortar.

The wall looks solid—but the materials are weak.

It appears sturdy—but it will collapse in the storm.

Their words sound convincing—but they are not rooted in truth.

God says: "There shall be an overflowing shower, and ye, O great hailstones, shall fall… and I will break down the wall that ye have daubed."

When the storm comes, the wall will fall.

And both the wall and the builders will be judged.

This is what false prophecy does:

> It builds fragile hope.

> It coats lies with spiritual language.

> It gives peace when there is no peace.

> It comforts rebellion and silences repentance.

But God sees through the plaster.

The Lie of Peace

> *"They have seduced My people, saying, Peace; and*
>
> *there was no peace."*
>
> *Ezekiel 13:10*

The central crime of these prophets is that they proclaimed peace when God had decreed judgment.

They anesthetized the people with flattery.

They dulled conviction with false reassurance.

They replaced warning with sentiment.

And the people believed them—because their words were easier to hear than Ezekiel's.

But the watchman must cry "sword" when the sword is coming.

He must declare fire when fire is at the door.

False prophets are beloved in moments of judgment because they offer illusion instead of instruction.

But their comfort is cruel.

Their hope is hollow.

Their words are weights that sink the soul.

God declares, "I am against you… your visions are vain, and your divinations are lies."

The Cursed Pillows and Kerchiefs

In verses 17–23, the Lord turns His attention to female false prophets—sorceresses who practiced manipulation and spiritual deception in the name of the Lord.

They sewed "pillows to all armholes" and made "kerchiefs upon the head of every stature," symbolizing occult coverings, seductive influence, and spiritual entrapment.

These were not simple headscarves. They were symbols of hidden power—tools of control, enchantment, and false protection.

God accuses them of:

- Hunting souls: using spiritual manipulation to control and ensnare others.
- Profaning Him among the people: twisting His Word for personal power.
- Killing the innocent and preserving the wicked: turning justice upside down through spiritual coercion.

They used God's name to cast spells, to deceive the vulnerable, and to trade in spiritual authority like currency.

God declares that He will tear off their coverings, deliver His people out of their hands, and make their lies powerless.

This is not just judgment. It is deliverance.

The Lord is rescuing His people from the grip of false religion.

The Weight of False Ministry

Ezekiel 13 is not simply a historical warning.

It is a mirror held up to every generation.

False prophecy still exists.

- It exists in pulpits that flatter sin and silence repentance.
- It exists in ministries that promise peace while ignoring purity.
- It exists in voices that speak often, but rarely weep.
- It exists in spiritual performance that lacks the fear of the Lord.

And just like in Ezekiel's day, these voices build walls—ministries, platforms, ideologies—that appear impressive, but are made of untempered mortar. When trial comes, the collapse is inevitable.

God is still against those who say, "Thus saith the Lord," when He has not spoken.

He is still against those who manipulate souls with charm, showmanship, and secret sin.

And He is still committed to exposing and dismantling every wall built on lies.

The Word and the Fire

The prophet Jeremiah spoke of this same danger:

> *"Is not My word like as a fire? saith the Lord; and like a hammer that breaketh the rock in pieces?"*
>
> *Jeremiah 23:29*

The true Word of the Lord is not a pillow.

It is a fire.

It is a hammer.

It does not flatter. It purifies.

The false prophet offers comfort.

The true prophet offers clarity.

The false prophet avoids offense.

The true prophet breaks the idols.

The false prophet protects the system.

The true prophet rends the veil.

Who Will Stand?

In every generation, God raises up Ezekiel's to confront the wall of lies.

But to stand against falsehood, one must fear God more than man.

The call is not to be harsh—but to be holy.

Not to be angry—but to be aligned.

Not to be loud—but to be faithful.

The wall is still being built.

The plaster is still being applied.

But the storm is approaching.

Will anyone cry out?

Will anyone tear down?

Will anyone tell the truth?

The Lord is still asking.

The Spirit is still searching.

Who will speak when He speaks?

Who will remain silent when He does not?

And who will stand—when the wall falls?

Chapter 9
The Heart of Stone and the Spirit Within

Ezekiel 36

The valley has been exposed.

The lies have been judged.

The glory has departed.

But in the dark stretch of prophetic grief, something shifts.

A new word emerges from the mouth of God—one not of wrath, but of restoration.

In Ezekiel 36, the tone turns. The divine fire does not vanish, but it is now aimed not at destruction—but at renewal.

God is no longer only dealing with the rebellion of His people; He is revealing His plan to resurrect them.

This chapter is the foundation of the new covenant—a promise that reaches beyond judgment and into the deepest chambers of the human soul.

Here, God promises what no ritual could achieve, what no prophet could command, what no law could force:

> *"A new heart also will I give you, and a new spirit will I put within you."*

This is the miracle that reforms history.

This is the beginning of resurrection.

The Mountains Will Speak Again

The chapter opens with a declaration to the land itself:

"Prophesy unto the mountains of Israel..."

God commands Ezekiel to speak not to kings, not to armies, not to priests—but to soil, rock, hills, and valleys.

Why?

Because the land had suffered.

It had been mocked by nations, trampled by enemies, left desolate.

But God had not forgotten it.

Even creation waits for redemption.

And so, before He addresses the heart of man, He addresses the heart of the land.

"The enemy hath said ... 'These ancient high places

are ours in possession."

But thus, saith the Lord God:

"Because they have made you desolate... I will lift up

My hand against them."

This is not nationalism.

This is covenant justice.

God is reclaiming what is His.

The land that bore the shame of exile will once again become fruitful.

The mountains that echoed with silence will once again hear the songs of the redeemed.

But the restoration of land is only the beginning.

The greater miracle is what God will do within.

"I Do This for My Holy Name's Sake"

Before outlining the promises of the new covenant, God makes one thing clear:

> *"I do not this for your sakes... but for Mine holy name's*
>
> *sake."*

This is the scandal of divine mercy:

God restores not because the people deserve it, but because His name has been defiled among the nations.

They bore His name—and yet they profaned it.

They were chosen—and yet they rebelled.

And yet God, in His sovereign mercy, will redeem them—not as a reward for repentance, but as a revelation of His holiness.

This is not grace without justice.

This is grace in spite of judgment.

The people failed.

The covenant was broken.

But God cannot deny Himself.

So, He will act—for His name.

He will sanctify Himself before the nations.

This is the first movement of the gospel:

God acts on behalf of His name, that His glory might be seen, even though broken vessels.

The Fourfold Promise

God outlines four miraculous promises—each one building upon

the next:

1. "Then will I sprinkle clean water upon you, and ye shall be clean…"
   This is the promise of purification. Not ceremonial, not symbolic—actual cleansing. From filth, from idols, from shame. God begins by washing away the past.
2. "A new heart also will I give you…"
   The old heart—hard, unresponsive, selfish—is removed. This is not behavioral modification. This is spiritual surgery. God replaces the core of man. The center of rebellion is taken out, and a tender, responsive heart is put in its place.
3. "And a new spirit will I put within you…"
   This is the internal ignition of life. A new animating force. A new direction. No longer bound to external commands, the soul is now awakened to divine desire.
4. "And I will put My Spirit within you…"

Not only a new heart, not only a new impulse, but God Himself

indwelling the human frame. This is the down payment of

Pentecost, the fulfillment of the promise. The same Spirit that

hovered over the waters now lives within the redeemed.

This fourfold promise is the blueprint of salvation.

It is the heart of the gospel—hidden in the scroll of the prophet.

God does not renovate the old nature.

He replaces it.

He does not simply command righteousness.

He enables it—from the inside out.

The Result: "Ye Shall Keep My Judgments"

This new heart is not merely emotional.

It is ethical.

The result of God's internal transformation is obedience.

> *"And cause you to walk in My statutes, and ye shall*
>
> *keep My judgments, and do them."*

Grace is not the absence of law.

Grace is the power to delight in it.

The law that once condemned now becomes the desire of the new heart.

This is the miracle of the Spirit:

We begin to want what God wants.

Not because we must.

But because we have been made new.

Desolation Reversed

The end of the chapter echoes the beginning.

The land will be tilled.

The ruined cities will be inhabited.

The nations will marvel.

And they will say:

> *"This land that was desolate is become like the garden*
>
> *of Eden."*

This is not mere geography.

It is prophetic symmetry.

Where there was curse, now there is blessing.

Where there was barrenness, now there is fruit.

Where there was judgment, now there is joy.

But none of this begins with land.

It begins with the heart.

A new Eden begins when a new spirit enters.

From Stone to Spirit

The heart of stone is still a plague in every generation.

It appears in rebellion.

It hardens in pride.

It resists the Word.

It covers itself in religion.

But God is still performing transplants.

He is still breathing into clay.

He is still pouring out His Spirit.

He is still making dead men live.

And when He does—The barren places bloom.

The ruined cities rise.

The Word becomes a song.

And the law becomes a joy.

This is not a distant dream.

It is the cry of now.

Let the stone be shattered.

Let the Spirit come in.

Let the heart live again.

THE VALLEY OF DRY BONES —
RESSURRECTION IN THE SPIRIT

Chapter 10
The Valley of Dry Bones —
Resurrection in the Spirit

Ezekiel 37:1–14

He had seen the glory.

He had witnessed the departure.

He had pronounced judgment and hoped for mercy.

But now, the Spirit takes him lower.

Before restoration comes, God leads Ezekiel not to a garden or a throne, but to a graveyard.

Not just a place of death—A place where even the memory of life has vanished.

> *"The hand of the Lord was upon me, and carried me*
> *out in the Spirit of the Lord, and set me down in the*
> *midst of the valley which was full of bones."*

This was not a battlefield.

The war was long over.

The bodies were not just lifeless—they were dismembered, sun-bleached, scattered.

This is not symbolic of sleep.

It is total desolation.

And the Spirit asks one of the most haunting questions in Scripture:

"Son of man, can these bones live?"

Not: Will they.

Not: Do you believe they might.

But: Can they?

Is resurrection even possible?

This is where true faith begins—In the face of impossible dryness.

"Can These Bones Live?"

Ezekiel answers with wisdom:

"O Lord God, Thou knowest."

He does not presume.

He does not pretend.

He does not formulate a strategy.

He simply yields to the One who holds the answer.

In doing so, he positions himself to become a vessel of the impossible.

Before God performs a miracle through a prophet, He often brings the prophet to the edge of hopelessness.

Ezekiel is not here to report on death.

He is here to call forth life.

The Command to Prophesy

"Prophesy upon these bones, and say unto them, O ye dry bones, hear the word of the Lord."

This command seems absurd.

Bones do not hear.

Death does not listen.

But the power of prophecy is not in the ears of the audience—

It is in the Word itself.

God does not need natural receptivity.

He needs obedient vessels.

Ezekiel speaks.

And as he speaks, something begins to happen:

> *"There was a noise, and behold a shaking, and the*
> *bones came together, bone to his bone."*

Structure returns.

Form returns.

Sinew, flesh, and skin cover the bones.

But there is still no breath.

It is possible to have structure without Spirit.

Form without function.

Order without life.

This is the danger of religious reconstruction without revival.

Everything appears in place—yet there is no breath.

And so, the Lord commands a second prophetic act.

"Prophecy to the Wind"

> *"Prophecy unto the wind... and say, Come from the*
> *four winds, O breath, and breathe upon these slain,*
> *that they may live."*

The first prophecy restores the body.

The second prophecy releases the breath.

The Hebrew word for "wind" here is ruach—the same word used for Spirit, breath, and wind throughout the Old Testament.

This is the breath of God that hovered over the waters in Genesis.

The wind that parted the Red Sea.

The Spirit that descended at Pentecost.

Ezekiel is not commanding air.

He is calling for the Spirit of resurrection.

And when the wind comes—

> *"They lived, and stood upon their feet, an exceeding*
> *great army."*

Not a crowd.

Not a congregation.

An army.

The bones that once lay scattered in silence now stand clothed with breath—ready to march.

This is not rehabilitation.

This is resurrection.

The House of Israel

God explains the vision plainly:

> *"Son of man, these bones are the whole house of*
>
> *Israel..."*

The people had said, "Our bones are dried, our hope is lost, we are cut off."

This was more than despair.

It was identity collapse.

They no longer saw themselves as God's people.

They had accepted the lie that their story had ended in exile.

But God disagreed.

> *"Behold, O My people, I will open your graves..."*

This is not only a metaphor for national restoration.

It is a declaration of divine power over every kind of death.

God does not merely encourage the downcast.

He resurrects the hopeless.

And He does so by His Word and His Spirit.

These two—proclamation and power—must always be joined.

Preaching without Spirit builds skeletons.

Spirit without Word creates chaos.

But when Word and Spirit come together—life appears.

From Grave to Glory

This valley is not merely about Israel.

It is about every generation that forgets who they are.

Every soul who feels scattered, lifeless, used up.

Every church that has form but no breath.

Every intercessor looking over a field of bones, wondering if revival is possible.

The answer is clear:

Yes. But only by the Spirit.

This vision is not a fable.

It is a blueprint.

Speak to the bones.

Call for the wind.

Watch the army rise.

This is the pattern of revival.

This is the movement of reformation.

This is the God who brings beauty from barrenness, soldiers from silence, breath from death.

Even now, the wind is waiting.

Chapter 11
The Two Sticks Become One —
The Unity of the Kingdom

Ezekiel 37:15–28

The bones have come together.

The breath has entered.

The army now stands.

But God is not finished.

Resurrection is not the end goal.

It is the beginning of something greater: restoration into unity.

For too long, the people of God had been divided—northern kingdom against southern, Ephraim against Judah, Samaria against Jerusalem. The exile had scattered them further. Their identity was fragmented. Their covenant inheritance was broken in half.

So, God gives Ezekiel a final sign in this chapter—not a valley, not a fire, not a sword, but a symbol made of wood.

"Take thee one stick, and write upon it, For Judah...

Then take another stick, and write upon it, For Joseph, the stick of Ephraim...

And join them one to another into one stick; and they shall become one in thine hand."

The prophet obeys. The sticks join. And the people ask, "Wilt thou not show us what thou meanest by these?"

God answers with clarity:

"Behold, I will take the children of Israel from among the heathen… and will bring them into their own land… and they shall be no more two nations… neither shall they be divided into two kingdoms any more at all."

This is not only a national promise.

It is a prophetic key.

God is not satisfied with revived people who remain divided.

The Pain of the Split

The division of the kingdoms—Judah in the south, Israel in the north—had existed since the days of Rehoboam and Jeroboam, nearly four centuries before Ezekiel's day.

The result had been devastating:

- Political instability.
- Competing worship systems.
- Mutual hatred.
- Loss of identity.
- Diminished witness.

Though both nations bore the covenant name, they walked in opposition.

This is the tragedy of division among the people of God:

Shared blood does not guarantee shared purpose.

Ezekiel's generation had inherited not only the consequences of sin but the long shadow of spiritual fragmentation.

Now, God says: Enough.

> *"I will make them one nation... and one King shall be*
> *King to them all."*

One Shepherd, One King

The language shifts from sticks and nations to a person:

> *"And David My servant shall be King over them; and*
> *they all shall have one Shepherd..."*

This is not a reference to the historical David.

It is a messianic prophecy—pointing forward to the Son of David, the true Shepherd-King, who would unite not only Israel and Judah but all peoples under His reign.

Jesus would later say:

> *"Other sheep I have, which are not of this fold: them*
> *also I must bring... and there shall be one fold, and one*
> *Shepherd."*
> *John 10:16*

Ezekiel 37 is not just about Israel.

It is about the church, the nations, the Bride, and the body of Christ.

It is about a fractured world healed under a righteous King.

This promise includes:

- One land.
- One King.
- One sanctuary.
- One everlasting covenant.
- One people of God.

The Language of Covenant

God reiterates the essence of His covenant with thunderous simplicity:

> *"I will be their God, and they shall be My people."*

This is the eternal goal of divine relationship.

Not only forgiveness, but fellowship.

Not only deliverance, but dwelling.

> *"My tabernacle also shall be with them… yea, I will be their God."*

The word "tabernacle" here points back to the wilderness, where God's glory filled the tent. But it also points forward—beyond the temple, beyond the exile, beyond Ezekiel—to Emmanuel, God with us.

> *"And the nations shall know that I the Lord do sanctify Israel, when My sanctuary shall be in the midst of them forevermore."*

This is not a mere geographic restoration.

It is a relational one.

The presence that departed in Ezekiel 10 will return.

The house will be filled again.

The covenant will be renewed.

But this time, the sanctuary will not be built with stone alone.

It will be built with hearts

From Division to Dwelling

The joining of the two sticks reveals the divine pattern:

1. Résurrections precedes réconciliation. God first brings life back to the bones—then unites what was broken.
2. Unity is not man-made. The prophet does not fuse the sticks by technique. He obeys, and God joins them in his hand.
3. Unity prepares the way for the King. Only once the sticks are joined does the King arise.

This is the order the Church must heed:

- Preach to the bones.
- Call for the wind.
- Join the sticks.
- Welcome the King.

Division in the body delays the glory.

Reconciliation in the Spirit prepares the house.

God will not dwell among fragmented altars.

He will reign where the people are one.

This is not superficial unity.

It is covenantal, spiritual, and holy.

It is not unity for unity's sake.

It is unity under one Shepherd, one covenant, one Spirit.

The Vision Today

We are still holding broken sticks.

Movements that do not speak to each other.

Denominations divided by walls God never built.

Nations separated by bitterness, fear, and mistrust.

But God is still saying:

"Take the sticks. Join them in your hand."

The power is not in the wood.

It is in the Word.

The prophet does not need to explain how.

He needs only to obey.

The miracle of unity is still possible.

But it will take prophets who are willing to hold broken pieces.

It will take shepherds who follow the Shepherd.

And it will take a Church that desires the presence of the King more than the preservation of its own name.

The bones have risen.

Now let the sticks be joined.

The King is near.

Chapter 12
Gog, Magog, and the
Final Invasion

Ezekiel 38–39

Resurrection has come.

The army stands.

The sticks are joined.

The sanctuary is promised.

And then—war.

Before the glory returns in fullness, before the temple is reestablished, a final confrontation erupts on the stage of history.

It is not a metaphor.

It is not a local skirmish.

It is cosmic in scale and eternal in meaning.

God reveals to Ezekiel one of the most mysterious and terrifying visions in all of prophetic Scripture: the battle of Gog and Magog.

Here, we see not only military strategy but spiritual enmity.

Not just nations in conflict, but the very forces of evil gathering for one last attempt to overthrow the purpose of God.

And God lets Ezekiel see it all—before it ever begins.

Who Is Gog? What Is Magog?

The chapter begins:

> *"Son of man, set thy face against Gog, the land of*
>
> *Magog, the chief prince of Meshech and Tubal..."*

Gog is not a nation, but a leader—a figure of immense military power, arrogance, and demonic alignment.

Magog is his territory—part of a coalition rooted in the far north.

Alongside Gog, other ancient regions are listed:

- Persia (modern Iran)
- Cush (Ethiopia/Sudan)
- Put (Libya)
- Gomer and Togarmah (regions in Asia Minor)

This coalition represents a confederation of nations—diverse in geography but united in hatred toward the people of God.

God says:

> *"I will turn thee back, and put hooks into thy jaws..."*

This detail is critical.

It is God Himself who draws Gog to war.

Not Satan. Not accident.

God sovereignly initiates the confrontation.

He draws out evil—not to empower it, but to destroy it once and for all.

This is divine strategy:

Expose the enemy fully before defeating him publicly.

"I Will Bring Thee Against My People"

Gog assembles his armies.

He descends like a storm upon the land of Israel.

His purpose: to devour, plunder, and erase.

But his timing is wrong.

God's people have returned.

They dwell in peace.

They are regathered by grace.

The enemy sees vulnerability.

God sees a trap.

> *"It shall come to pass at the same time... that My fury*
> *shall come up in My face."*
> *Ezekiel 38:18*

The God who was once silent is now stirred.

He speaks with fury.

He moves with fire.

This is not an act of defensive protection.

It is holy war—led by the King of Glory Himself.

Earthquakes shake the land.

Mountains are thrown down.

Pestilence, blood, hail, fire, and brimstone fall from the sky.

The coalition is crushed not by Israel's army, but by God's own hand.

> *"And I will be known in the eyes of many nations, and*
> *they shall know that I am the Lord."*
> *Ezekiel 38:23*

This is not just a military victory.

It is a revelation of divine sovereignty.

God proves to the nations—and to Israel—that He alone is King.

The Aftermath: Seven Years of Cleansing

In Ezekiel 39, the aftermath unfolds in staggering detail:

- The weapons of the fallen army are gathered and burned for seven years.
- The land is so littered with corpses that it takes seven months to bury the dead.
- A special valley is set aside—the valley of Hamon-Gog—for the mass graves.

This is not exaggeration.

It is biblical realism.

Ezekiel is seeing a day when the enemies of God are utterly

overthrown, and the land itself must undergo cleansing.

The image is both horrifying and holy.

God's wrath is not petty.

It is purifying.

The land must be washed of blood.

The people must see the cost of rebellion.

And the world must witness the supremacy of the Lord.

> *"So the house of Israel shall know that I am the Lord*
> *their God from that day and forward."*
> *Ezekiel 39:22*

This is re-covenanting through fire.

Israel will no longer question.

The nations will no longer mock.

The Lord will no longer be hidden.

He will be known.

Theological Meaning of Gog and Magog

The battle of Gog and Magog is not just geopolitical.

It is eschatological—pointing toward the final alignment of evil before the full reign of Christ.

The same names—Gog and Magog—appear again in Revelation 20:8, after the millennial reign of Christ, in one last demonic uprising before the final judgment.

Whether these are two separate battles or one pattern repeated across ages, the message is the same:

Evil always gathers for one final strike—And God always answers with absolute finality.

Gog represents:

- The pride of man.
- The rebellion of nations.
- The spiritual hostility toward covenant.
- The last gasp of darkness before everlasting light.

And Magog is the staging ground of this rebellion.

But God is not intimidated.

He draws them out.

He exposes them fully.

And He silences them forever.

Why This Vision Matters Now

Ezekiel 38–39 reminds us that peace is not the absence of war—it is the presence of God's sovereignty.

We are not promised a smooth history.

We are promised a righteous end.

Nations will rage.

Alliances will form.

Leaders will rise with the voice of Gog.

But God's hand is steady.

His eye is not blind.

And His fury is not asleep.

This chapter is a warning—But it is also a comfort.

The people of God may be surrounded—But they are never
outnumbered

The enemy may advance—But his steps are already written into the
scroll of defeat.

The hooks are in his jaw.

The trap has been laid.

The glory is preparing to return.

Let every intercessor take heart.

Let every watchman stay awake.

Let every saint lift their head.

The Sovereign Lord is still in command.

The King will have the final word.

And the nations shall know that He is the Lord.

CHAPTER 13

THE VISION OF THE TEMPLE – MEASUREMENTS OF GLORY

EZEKIEL 40–42

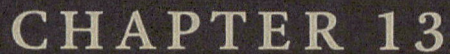

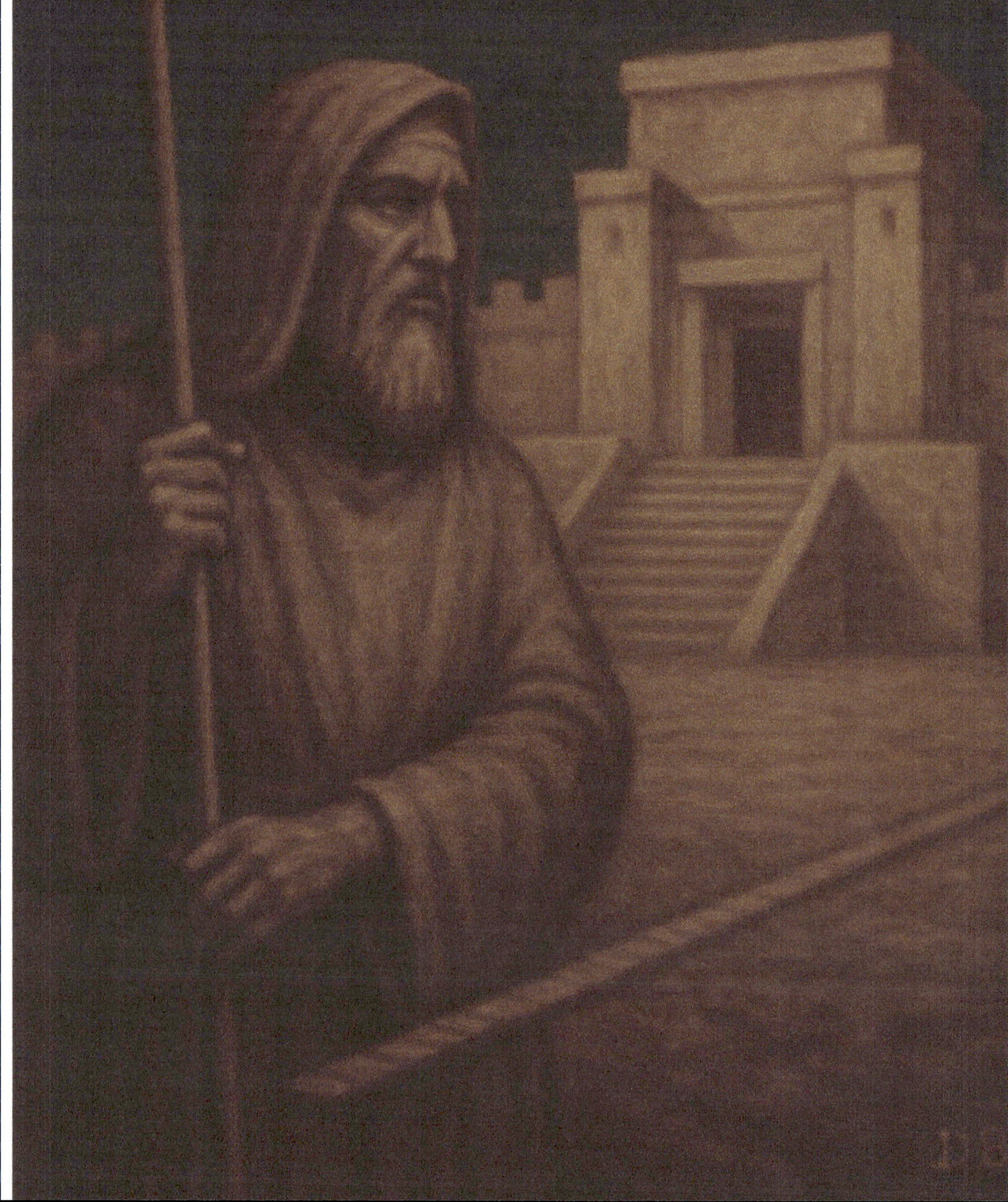

Chapter 13
The Vision of the Temple —
Measurements of Glory

Ezekiel 40–42

The battlefield is quiet.

The bones have risen.

The enemy has been crushed.

The land is being cleansed.

And then—a new vision begins.

In the twenty-fifth year of the exile, fourteen years after the city of Jerusalem was destroyed, the hand of the Lord comes upon Ezekiel once more.

But this time, He does not show him bones or armies.

He shows him a building.

A temple.

A structure not yet built, a sanctuary untouched by Babylon, a design etched not by human architects but by the hand of God.

This is no ordinary blueprint.

This is a heavenly measurement—a sacred geometry of restoration.

And the prophet becomes a surveyor of the future.

> *"In the visions of God brought He me into the land of Israel, and set me upon a very high mountain..."*

Here begins the final section of the book: the temple vision, spanning chapters 40 through 48.

It is the longest, most detailed temple description in the Bible—and it is not for nostalgia. It is prophetic revelation.

God is not restoring the past.

He is revealing the dimensions of where His glory will dwell again.

The Man with the Measuring Reed

Ezekiel sees a man "whose appearance was like brass," standing in the gateway with a line of flax in one hand and a measuring reed in the other.

This is a divine messenger—part angel, part architect, assigned to guide Ezekiel through the measurements of this future house.

Every detail matters. Every length is recorded. Every threshold is examined.

The Lord is not interested in building something symbolic.

He is laying out the specifics of a real, holy place.

This is the language of reverence:

God measures before He fills.

He designs before He dwells.

The message is clear:

The glory of God will not inhabit what is not prepared.

Just as Noah's ark had dimensions,

Just as the tabernacle had blueprints,

Just as Solomon's temple was constructed according to exact patterns So, too will this temple be built to perfection—because it is not a monument to man's effort, but a home for God's presence.

Why So Many Measurements?

To the casual reader, Ezekiel 40–42 can seem technical—cubits, gates, porches, chambers, altars.

But in prophetic literature, measurements are never meaningless.

They convey two things:

1. Divine Order — Every inch reveals that God is not improvising. He is restoring by plan. What was defiled by idolatry will now be rebuilt with precision.
2. Divine Ownership — The measuring reed is a claim of possession. God is saying, "This is Mine. This is where I will dwell. No corruption will enter here again."

The structure is not random.

It is prophetic architecture—mirroring holiness, access, and consecration.

Every chamber, every court, every stairway tells the story of a God returning to a holy house.

Eastward Orientation

The temple is oriented toward the east—the direction from which the glory will return.

This is not accidental.

The east was the gate of Eden.

The east was the direction of exile.

And now, the east will become the entry point of restoration.

The house faces the rising sun.

It awaits the return of the light.

It watches for the King.

God is building a house that anticipates His presence.

This is the theology of hope made architectural.

Sacred Separation

The temple vision also outlines multiple zones of sacred separation:

- The outer court, where the people may gather.

- The inner court, reserved for priests.

- The most holy place, where only the High Priest may enter.

These zones are not about elitism.

They are about holiness.

God is making a statement: Access to My glory must be honored.

This sacred arrangement was not abolished by grace—it was fulfilled

in Christ, who tore the veil. But the principle remains:

God's presence is weighty. It is not casual.

In a day of spiritual informality, this vision reminds us:

The closer we come to His glory,

the deeper our reverence must grow.

The Priestly Chambers

The vision continues with detailed instructions for chambers

where the priests shall change garments, offer sacrifices, and eat the

holy portion.

There are laws for purification.

Spaces for consecration.

Rooms for rest and renewal.

The message is implicit:

Ministers of God must be set apart.

God does not allow His servants to move between sacred and

common without transition.

Even the garments matter.

This is not legalism.

It is reverence.

It is the way of holiness.

The modern Church must recover this balance:

Closeness with God requires consecration.

The Walls and the Thresholds

Walls surround the entire structure—thick, fortified, defined.

Thresholds are clearly marked.

Doors swing in order.

Space is assigned with purpose.

Why?

Because boundaries protect glory.

In the previous temple, idols were placed near the threshold.

Secret sin had crept into holy space.

But not this time.

God is restoring a house with walls that guard, gates that welcome, and thresholds that sanctify.

His glory will not dwell in a house without boundaries.

This vision is a blueprint for holiness.

It speaks not only of a building to come, but of a people being prepared.

A House Ready for Glory

These three chapters—Ezekiel 40 through 42—do not yet mention the return of the glory.

They only show the preparation.

But that in itself is the message:

God reveals the structure before He returns His Spirit.

Ezekiel is made to walk every hallway, measure every gate, observe every chamber.

The vision slows down here.

The Spirit lingers.

Because this is the place where Heaven will meet earth again.

It must be right.

Before revival, there must be order.

Before the cloud descends, the house must be ready.

This is a call to the modern Church:

- Rebuild the altars.
- Redraw the boundaries.
- Measure the threshold.
- Prepare the house.

The glory is near.

But it will not return to chaos.

God is giving us the reed.

Let us build what He is measuring.

THE GLORY RETURNS
THE KING ENTERS AGAIN
Ezekiel 43

DE

Chapter 14
The Glory Returns — The King
Enters Again

Ezekiel 43

He saw it leave.

He watched it rise from the threshold.

He followed it to the eastern gate.

He stood in silence as the glory of the Lord lifted from the city and ascended to the mountain.

But now, years later, standing before a newly measured temple,

Ezekiel sees what few have ever seen:

The glory returns.

> *"Afterward he brought me to the gate, even the gate*
>
> *that looketh toward the east: And, behold, the glory of*
>
> *the God of Israel came from the way of the east..."*
>
> *(Ezekiel 43:1–2)*

The same direction from which it departed—The same path it took to leave—Is now the route of return.

God is faithful not only to dwell,

But to come back.

This is not a different glory.

It is the same glory Ezekiel saw at the river Chebar.

The same glory that once rested on the ark.

The same glory that filled Solomon's temple.

Now it returns—with a sound like many waters.

And the prophet, overcome, does what he did in the beginning:

"And I fell upon my face."

This is how you know the real glory has come.

It produces no performance.

Only reverence.

From Departure to Return

The journey of the glory in Ezekiel forms a full arc:

- Ezekiel 10–11: The glory departs.
- Ezekiel 43: The glory returns.

In both cases, it moves eastward.

But what makes the return so profound is not just that God comes back—It's how He comes back.

He returns not in wrath, but in radiance.

Not in judgment, but in dwelling.

Not to destroy, but to fill.

This is the fulfillment of God's covenant heart:

"My tabernacle also shall be with them... and I will be

their God."

Ezekiel 37:27

The return of the glory signals that God has chosen to live among His people again.

Not from a distance.

Not in theory.

But in fullness.

The Voice From the House

As the glory enters the eastern gate and fills the inner court, Ezekiel hears a voice—not from heaven, but from inside the house:

"Son of man, the place of My throne, and the place of the soles of My feet, where I will dwell in the midst of the children of Israel for ever..."

This declaration is unlike any spoken before.

God does not say, "I will visit,"

but "I will dwell."

Not temporarily.

Permanently.

"...and My holy name shall the house of Israel no more defile..."

The return of the glory is conditional on holiness.

Where sin once stood, purity must reign.

Where compromise once flourished, consecration must be restored.

God is not returning to visit a corrupt house.

He is returning to inhabit a consecrated one.

This is not revival without repentance.

It is revival through repentance.

Measure the Pattern

Then the Lord gives Ezekiel a final charge:

"Show the house to the house of Israel... that they may be ashamed of their iniquities: and let them measure the pattern."
Ezekiel 43:10

The very structure of the temple is meant to produce conviction.

The walls are holy.

The gates are precise.

The altar is exact.

When the people see what God has designed, they will compare it to what they built—and be ashamed.

This is not condemnation.

It is invitation.

When the pattern of heaven is revealed, earthly imitation must yield.

When God's measurements are shown, man's distortions must fall.

The modern Church must ask:

Have we measured the pattern?

Have we built what He revealed?

Or have we plastered our own blueprints over His?

God does not fill what He has not designed.

If we want His glory, we must re-measure the house.

The Altar Is Restored

At the heart of the restored temple is the altar.

God gives Ezekiel detailed instructions for its dimensions, steps, and consecration.

This is no casual platform.

This is the place of fire.

> *"And the altar shall be eight cubits high... and the*
> *hearth shall be four cubits..."*

Every inch is recorded.

Every offering is assigned.

Why?

Because worship must be ordered before it can be received.

This altar will not be used for show.

It will not be offered on by defiled hands.

Only the sons of Zadok—those who remained faithful—will serve here.

Only what is pure will be accepted.

The glory of God requires the altar of God to be restored.

No altar, no fire.

No fire, no presence.

No presence, no purpose.

The Glory in Our Generation

Ezekiel's vision is not just about a temple.

It is about the God who fills it.

Today, we long for revival.

We pray for glory.

We hunger for His return.

But the pattern has not changed:

- The house must be measured.
- The altar must be restored.
- The priests must be consecrated.
- And the gate must face east—in expectation of the King.

The glory will return.

Not to entertain, but to dwell.

Not to pass by, but to inhabit.

Let the watchmen proclaim it.

Let the builders prepare.

Let the people fall on their faces.

The King is at the gate.

Chapter 15
Holy Offerings and
Priestly Order

Ezekiel 44–46

The glory has returned.

The King has entered through the eastern gate.

The house has been measured.

The altar has been rebuilt.

Now comes the question:

Who will minister in the presence of this glory?

Who will draw near? Who will handle the holy?

Ezekiel 44 through 46 answers this question with unshakable clarity.

God is no longer addressing the external structure—He is
addressing the internal posture of those who would stand
before Him.

These chapters restore what was once defiled:

The priesthood.

The offerings.

The rhythm of worship.

The sanctity of sacred space.

No longer will anyone enter casually.

No longer will ministers serve for status.

No longer will offerings be treated as common.

The house is now filled with glory—And only those who fear the Lord will be allowed to serve within it.

The Closed Gate and the Prince

"Then He brought me back the way of the gate of the

outward sanctuary which looketh toward the east;

and it was shut."

"Then said the Lord unto me; This gate shall be shut, it

shall not be opened... because the Lord, the God of

Israel, hath entered in by it..."

(Ezekiel 44:1–2)

The eastern gate, the path of the King, is now sealed.

Why?

Because once the Lord has entered, no one else may tread that path.

This is a divine act of honor and separation.

The King's procession is not repeated.

The gate becomes a monument of majesty—preserved for His glory alone.

And yet, a mysterious figure appears: "the prince."

He is not the Messiah, but a representative leader—one who rules in righteousness, enters by the vestibule, and eats bread before the Lord.

This prince honors the King but does not replace Him.

He leads in humility, not exaltation.

He approaches, but never overshadows.

The message is clear:

Leadership in the house of God must honor the path of the glory—not compete with it.

The Sons of Zadok

Then the Lord makes a distinction among the priests:

> *"But the priests the Levites, the sons of Zadok… they*
>
> *shall come near to Me, to minister unto Me."*

This distinction is historical and holy.

When Israel went astray, the Levites compromised—ministering to idols and serving the people instead of guarding the sanctity of the temple.

But the sons of Zadok remained faithful.

They stood with David.

They guarded the ark.

They ministered to the Lord when others catered to the crowd.

And so now, in this restored house, only the faithful shall serve in the inner court.

They shall:

- Wear linen, not wool—so they do not sweat in God's presence.
- Not shave their heads or grow their hair long—remaining balanced in appearance.
- Teach the people the difference between holy and profane.
- Judge controversies with justice.
- Keep God's Sabbaths and walk in His statutes.

These priests are guardians of glory, not performers of ritual.

They carry the weight of reverence.

They uphold the standard of holiness.

God is not interested in titles.

He is interested in fidelity.

The restored priesthood is not based on lineage alone, but on loyalty.

The Offerings Restored

Chapters 45 and 46 outline the reinstatement of offerings in the temple:

- Burnt offerings
- Sin offerings
- Peace offerings
- Grain offerings
- Drink offerings
- Sabbaths and feasts

At first glance, this may seem like a return to the Mosaic system.

But something deeper is at work.

These offerings are not about atonement.

They are about honor.

The people are no longer offering under fear of wrath.

They are offering under the weight of worship.

God reestablishes the Sabbath offerings, the New Moon sacrifices, the Passover observance, and the daily oblation.

Each offering is measured.

Each one is exact.

Each is a response to the glory that now fills the house.

> *"And in the feasts and in the solemnities the meat offering shall be an ephah to a bullock... and the drink offering shall be a hin of oil to an ephah."*
> *(Ezekiel 45:24)*

These are not burdens.

They are sacred rhythms—acts of remembrance, gratitude, and celebration.

In the restored temple, worship is not an event.

It is a way of life.

Justice and Holiness in Leadership

Ezekiel 45:9 includes a rebuke and a command:

> *"Let it suffice you, O princes of Israel: remove violence*
> *and spoil, and execute judgment and justice..."*

The leaders are commanded to stop oppressing the people.

Their weights and balances must be just.

Their measurements must be honest.

Why?

Because the presence of God demands equity.

No corruption can be hidden beneath liturgy.

No injustice can coexist with incense.

God is rebuilding a society where the throne of glory is matched by a culture of justice.

The house cannot be holy if the land is dishonest.

The River of Worship

Ezekiel 46 ends with a description of the people's movement in worship:

> *"But when the people of the land shall come before the*
> *Lord in the solemn feasts, he that entereth in by the*
> *north gate... shall go forth by the south gate..."*

They cannot exit the same way they entered.

They must pass through.

Why?

Because true worship changes direction.

You leave differently than you came.

You are transformed by the encounter.

Even in architecture, God teaches transformation.

Worship is not a loop.

It is a passage.

You meet the Lord, and you are never the same.

Preparing the House Today

The message is clear:

If the glory has returned:

Then the house must be ordered.

The priests must be faithful.

The offerings must be holy.

The leaders must be just.

And the people must walk in reverence.

This is not law.

This is love.

This is the way a people live when the Lord is actually among them.

This is not nostalgia for the old covenant.

It is prophecy of the millennial reign, A glimpse of the kingdom to come—Where Jesus reigns, Where worship is pure, Where every gate faces east, And every altar burns with sacred fire.

Let us prepare.

The glory is not theoretical.

It is personal. It is coming.

THE LORD IS A
PRECISE
REDEEMER
JUDAH
REUBEN
ISSACHAR
DAN
SIMEON
NAPHTALI
REUBEN
EPHRAIM
ISSACHAR
BENJAMIN
MANASSEH
ZEBULUN
EZEKIEL 47:13

Chapter 16
The River from the Altar —
Healing for the Nations

Ezekiel 47:1–12

The altar has been consecrated.

The priests have been purified.

The offerings have been restored.

The house has been filled with glory.

Now Ezekiel sees something more.

From the threshold of the temple, from beneath the place of sacrifice, a river begins to flow.

It is not poured out.

It is not summoned.

It simply appears—silent at first, then rising.

This is not a stream dug by man.

This is living water—originating not from rain or springs, but from the presence of God Himself.

And it flows eastward.

Toward the direction of exile.

Toward the valley of dry bones.

Toward the desert, the dead sea, and the nations.

Because the glory that returns to the temple will not remain locked within it.

God is not rebuilding a house to contain His presence,

but to release it.

A Measured River

Ezekiel is led through this water by a man with a measuring line:

"He brought me through the waters; the waters were

to the ankles... to the knees... to the loins...

then waters to swim in, a river that could not be

passed over."

Ezekiel 47:3–5

Every thousand cubits, the water rises.

Why?

Because God increases by measure.

He does not overwhelm all at once.

He invites the faithful step by step.

He brings the prophet in slowly—until he cannot stand anymore,

until he must surrender and swim.

This is a picture of spiritual progression:

- Ankle-deep — You feel the Spirit.
- Knee-deep — You begin to pray.
- Waist-deep — You yield more.
- Over your head — You are no longer in control.
  You float in the current of glory.

The farther you go from the temple, the deeper the water gets.

This is no contradiction.

It is divine design.

The temple is the source.

But the movement is outward.

The Spirit is not meant to pool. It is meant to flow.

Wherever the river goes, life follows.

Healing the Dead Sea

The river flows east toward the Arabah—the wilderness valley—and enters the Dead Sea.

This is the lowest point on earth.

A body of water with no outlet, high in salt, sterile to life.

But when the river reaches it—

it is healed.

> *"These waters issue out... into the sea: which being brought forth into the sea, the waters shall be healed."*
> *"And it shall come to pass, that every thing that liveth... whithersoever the rivers shall come, shall live."*
> *Ezekiel 47:8–9*

This is resurrection.

This is reversal.

This is the power of God's presence to restore what was declared dead.

No sea is too salty.

No valley too dry.

No region too far.

The river touches it—and life multiplies.

Fishermen stand on its banks.

Fruit trees grow beside it.

Leaves heal.

Waters teem with life.

This is more than a metaphor.

It is a prophetic promise.

Wherever the Spirit flows—Nations are healed. Cities are awakened.

People are reborn.

The River and the Spirit

This river is not only a vision of water.

It is a vision of the Holy Spirit.

In the last days, Jesus stood and cried:

> *"If any man thirst, let him come unto Me, and drink...*
>
> *out of his belly shall flow rivers of living water.*
>
> *(But this spake He of the Spirit...)"*
>
> *John 7:37–39*

Ezekiel saw it in vision.

Jesus fulfilled it in flesh.

The Church is now called to release it.

The altar—Christ.

The temple—His Body.

The threshold—our hearts.

The river—His Spirit.

And the direction?

Always outward.

This is not a call to build better sanctuaries.

It is a call to let the river flow.

Revival is not for us alone.

It is for the broken, the distant, the dead seas of this generation.

But it must begin at the altar.

No altar, no flow.

No sacrifice, no Spirit.

No presence, no power.

The Church must return to the threshold—Not for performance, but for outpouring.

The Trees Beside the River

Along both banks of the river grow trees bearing fruit each month:

> *"Their leaf shall not fade, neither shall the fruit*
>
> *thereof be consumed:*
>
> *it shall bring forth new fruit according to his months...*
>
> *and the fruit thereof shall be for meat, and the leaf*
>
> *thereof for medicine."*
>
> *(Ezekiel 47:12)*

This image reappears in Revelation 22:

> *"On either side of the river... was the tree of life... and*
>
> *the leaves of the tree were for the healing of the*
>
> *nations."*

From Genesis to Ezekiel to Revelation, the river is present.

It flowed through Eden.

It flows from the altar.

It flows from the throne of God and the Lamb.

This is God's eternal design—A people rooted by the river, bearing fruit in every season, healing nations by what flows through them.

These trees represent you and me.

Planted. Fed. Yielding. Healing.

Not by talent.

Not by strategy.

But by the river of God.

A Church by the Water

In the vision of Ezekiel, the Church is not described by its programs or positions.

It is described by its flow.

Are we ankle-deep?

Knee-deep?

Or surrendered to the river?

Do we measure our success by numbers—Or by the depth of our healing waters?

God is not looking for larger temples.

He is looking for open thresholds.

From the altar to the nations—Let the Spirit flow.

Let the Church be a river again.

Let dead places live.

Let the fishermen gather.

Let the fruit bear.

Let the nations be healed.

The Inheritance and the Eternal Land

Ezekiel 47:13–48:35

The visions are nearly complete.

The glory has returned.

The river flows with healing.

The house is consecrated.

And now—the final act:

The land is divided.

What began in judgment ends in justice.

What began in exile ends in inheritance.

God does not merely restore the temple.

He restores the land, the tribes, the boundaries, and the identity of
His people.

This is not symbolic.

It is specific.

Lines are drawn.

Borders are measured.

Names are restored.

Twelve tribes—each with a portion.

Each re-rooted in the land of promise.

The same people once scattered by sin
are now gathered by grace.

The Lord Is a Precise Redeemer

Ezekiel 47:13 begins with divine instructions for the land:

> *"Thus saith the Lord God; This shall be the border,*
> *whereby ye shall inherit the land according to the*
> *twelve tribes of Israel..."*

Each tribe is named.

Each boundary is drawn from the north to the south.

This is a prophetic reversal of the exile.

What was lost is now returned.

What was desolate is now defined.

What was once occupied by foreign powers is now sanctified by
divine presence.

Even the strangers who sojourn in the land—those not born of
Israel—are given inheritance if they dwell and walk among God's
people (Ezekiel 47:22–23).

This is not nationalism.

This is covenantal inclusion.

God is not just reestablishing borders—He is rebuilding belonging.

The Sacred Portion

At the center of the land lies a holy allotment—set aside for the Lord Himself:

> *"Moreover, when ye shall divide by lot the land for*
> *inheritance, ye shall offer an oblation unto the Lord,*
> *an holy portion of the land..."*
>
> *Ezekiel 45:1*

This sacred portion includes:

- The sanctuary (temple)
- The land for the priests and Levites
- The land for the city and the prince
- Fields and provisions for the workers of the sanctuary

Every class of people is considered.

Every need is remembered.

Every portion is measured in holiness.

This is not just a territory.

It is a tabernacle society—centered on the Lord, surrounded by justice, upheld by righteousness.

Even the prince, who once ruled with corruption, is now held in accountability:

> *"He shall not take of the people's inheritance by*
> *oppression... out of his own possession shall he give*
> *inheritance to his sons."*
>
> *Ezekiel 46:18*

Leadership is no longer about power.

It is about stewardship under the shadow of glory.

The Gates of the City

Finally, Ezekiel sees the city.

Its name?

Not Jerusalem.

Not Zion.

Not the New City.

Its name is a revelation:

> *"...and the name of the city from that day shall be,*
>
> *The Lord is there."*
>
> *Ezekiel 48:35*

Hebrew: YHWH Shammah — יהוה שמה

> *"The Lord is Present"*

This is not just geography.

This is theology.

This is destiny.

The deepest ache of exile has been healed.

The cry "Ichabod" (the glory has departed) is now silenced.

In its place, a city named after the abiding presence of God.

Twelve gates surround the city—each named for a tribe of Israel.

Three gates on each side: north, south, east, and west.

The people are re-gathered from every direction.

The city is accessible from every side.

And at the center of it all—YHWH Shammah.

He is not afar.

He is not passing through.

He is there.

The Eternal Pattern

This final vision connects to a larger narrative—a divine pattern that stretches from Eden to Revelation:

- In Eden, man walked with God.
- In the Tabernacle, He dwelt in their midst.
- In the Temple, His glory filled the house.
- In Ezekiel, His glory returns to a purified people.
- In Revelation, the dwelling of God is with men again—forever.

Ezekiel's city is a shadow of eternity.

John would later see it:

> *"And I saw no temple therein: for the Lord God*
>
> *Almighty and the Lamb are the temple of it...*
>
> *and the nations of them which are saved shall walk in*
>
> *the light of it..."*
>
> *Revelation 21:22–24*

This is the destination.

Not just land—but presence.

Not just inheritance—but union.

Not just restoration—but consummation.

Ezekiel has walked through judgment, through exile, through visions of wheels and fire, through lament and command, through temple measurements and priestly orders, through rivers and trees and boundaries and gates—All to bring us to this one truth:

The Lord is there.

Not in part.

Not in passing.

But in fullness.

Forever.

From the Watchman's Window

You have now seen through Ezekiel's window.

You've watched the glory depart and return.

You've measured the house.

You've walked the river.

You've heard the voice.

But now, the time has come to stand in the vision. We are not called to merely interpret Ezekiel.

We are called to embody it:

- To be priests like Zadok
- To live near the altar
- To carry the fire
- To release the river
- To await the return of the King

The house is ready.

The gates are facing east. The throne is in place. And the cry of the Spirit still echoes—"The Lord is there."

Conclusion

When the Watchman Becomes the Vision

Ezekiel began as a captive—a priest in exile,

a man of heritage without a temple, a voice crying among the bones

of Babylon.

He sat among the displaced, by the river Chebar, when the heavens

opened and visions of God broke through the clouds.

He saw wheels.

He saw fire.

He saw the glory depart.

And then he was made a watchman.

Not a scribe.

Not a priest of ritual.

But a seer of the Spirit.

He was told to eat the scroll.

To speak only when God opened his mouth.

To lay on his side.

To bear prophetic burdens in public.

To cry aloud.

To act out signs.

To deliver the Word of the Lord when no one would listen.

And for twenty-two years—he watched.

He watched Jerusalem fall.

He watched false prophets rise.

He watched the temple burn.

He watched the elders compromise.

He watched the bones of the nation dry and scatter.

But he also watched the glory return.

He watched the temple measured, the altar rebuilt, the river flow, the land restored, and the name of the city change forever:

YHWH Shammah — The LORD is there.

This is more than a historical account.

This is the final lens of the watchman:

A lens not fixed on the past, but burning with future light.

Because what Ezekiel saw is what the Church must now become.

We are not in exile from Babylon—but we live in a world just as fractured, just as pagan, just as blind.

We too have seen the house of God defiled.

We too have heard false voices speak in His name.

We too have wandered from holiness.

We too long for the glory to return.

And so the Lord is raising up Ezekiel's once again—Not to perform, but to prophesy.

Not to condemn, but to call back.

Not to flatter, but to reveal.

Not to decorate religion, but to unveil reality.

You, reader, are not meant to merely read this book.

You are meant to become a watchman.

Not one who sits in comfort,

but one who watches by day and night.

One who warns with tears.

One who cries over compromise.

One who stands in the breach.

One who dreams, fasts, intercedes, and measures the sanctuary with sacred hands.

Ezekiel never got to rebuild the temple.

But he laid the pattern.

He never lived to walk in the restored land.

But he saw its boundaries.

He never stood in the New Jerusalem.

But he received its name.

And you, child of God, now hold the scroll he ate.

Will you watch?

Will you speak?

Will you weep over what God weeps for?

Will you fall on your face when the glory returns?

Will you measure the altar?

Will you let the river rise from your feet to your spirit?

Will you be marked among the faithful who mourn over the defilement in the land?

Because now is the time.

The days of dull religion are ending.

The King is returning.

The eastern gate is opening.

Let the watchmen rise.

Let the priests of Zadok come forward.

Let the house be measured.

Let the river flow.

Let the exiles return.

Let the name of the city be declared:

"The LORD is there."

Scripture Index
Scripture References by Chapter

Chapter 1 – The Heavens Opened

- Ezekiel 1:1–28
- Revelation 4:2–6
- Isaiah 6:1–7

Chapter 2 – The Scroll and the Call

- Ezekiel 2:1–10
- Ezekiel 3:1–27
- Jeremiah 15:16
- Revelation 10:9–10

Chapter 3 – The Watchman's Burden

- Ezekiel 3:16–21
- Ezekiel 33:1–9
- Isaiah 62:6
- Acts 20:26–27

Chapter 4 – The Departing Glory

- Ezekiel 8:1–18
- Ezekiel 9:3; 10:1–22
- Ezekiel 11:22–23
- 1 Samuel 4:21
- John 1:14

Chapter 5 – Judgment Begins at the Sanctuary

- Ezekiel 9:1–11
- 1 Peter 4:17
- Revelation 2:5

Chapter 6 – A Prophetic Sign to a Rebellious House

- Ezekiel 4:1–17
- Ezekiel 5:1–17
- Ezekiel 12:1–16

Chapter 7 – The Mountains of Israel and the Idols of the Heart

- Ezekiel 6:1–14
- Ezekiel 14:1–11
- Isaiah 2:18
- Matthew 5:8

Chapter 8 – The Shepherds and the Scattered Sheep

- Ezekiel 34:1–31
- John 10:11–16
- Psalm 23:1

Chapter 9 – The New Heart and the New Spirit

- Ezekiel 36:22–32
- Jeremiah 31:33
- John 3:5–8
- Titus 3:5

Chapter 10 – The Valley of Dry Bones — Resurrection in the Spirit

- Ezekiel 37:1–14
- John 11:25
- Romans 8:11
- Revelation 11:11

Chapter 11 – The Two Sticks Become One — The Unity of the Kingdom

- Ezekiel 37:15–28
- John 17:21–23
- Isaiah 11:12–13

Chapter 12 – Gog and Magog — The Final Conflict

- Ezekiel 38–39
- Revelation 20:7–10
- Zechariah 12:9
- Joel 3:2

Chapter 13 – The Temple of the Lord

- Ezekiel 40–43
- 1 Corinthians 3:16–17
- Revelation 11:1

Chapter 14 – The Priesthood of Zadok — A Holy Remnant

- Ezekiel 44:15–31
- Malachi 3:3
- Revelation 1:6

Chapter 15 – The Altar and the Glory Returned

- Ezekiel 43:1–12
- Exodus 29:36–43
- Hebrews 13:10–12

Chapter 16 – The River from the Altar — Healing for the Nations

- Ezekiel 47:1–12
- Revelation 22:1–2
- John 7:37–39

Chapter 17 – The Inheritance and the Eternal Land

- Ezekiel 47:13–48:35
- Revelation 21:1–3
- Isaiah 60:18

Glossary of Terms

Altar – The sacred place of sacrifice in the temple, representing atonement, worship, and the presence of God. In Ezekiel, the altar is restored as the source from which the river of life flows.

Apocalyptic Literature – A genre of Scripture that reveals divine mysteries through visions, symbols, and prophetic imagery, especially related to judgment and restoration.

Chebar River – The river in Babylon near which Ezekiel received his visions. Symbolic of exile, but also the location of divine revelation.

Ezekiel – A priest turned prophet during the Babylonian exile, called to be a watchman over Israel. His book contains visions of judgment, restoration, and the glory of God.

Glory of the Lord (Hebrew: Kavod YHWH) – The visible manifestation of God's presence, often described as radiant light or fire. In Ezekiel, the glory departs and later returns to the temple.

Gog and Magog – Mysterious prophetic enemies of Israel mentioned in Ezekiel 38–39 and Revelation 20, representing the final rebellion against God before the establishment of His eternal reign.

Holy Portion – The central section of the land set aside for the sanctuary, the priests, the city, and the prince. Represents the centrality of God's presence in restored society.

Ichabod – A term meaning "the glory has departed," reflecting the spiritual desolation that occurs when God's presence is removed.

Ruach – Hebrew word meaning breath, wind, or spirit. Used in Ezekiel to describe both the Spirit of God and the breath that revives the dry bones.

Shammah (YHWH Shammah) –"The Lord is There"; the final name given to the city in Ezekiel's vision, signifying God's permanent presence with His people.

The Watchman – Ezekiel's divine calling. A spiritual guardian appointed to warn the people of God's coming judgment or to proclaim His restoration.

The Zadok Priesthood – A faithful remnant of priests from the line of Zadok who are called to minister before the Lord in holiness, in contrast to those who led Israel astray.

Temple Vision – Ezekiel's detailed vision of a future temple, beginning in Ezekiel 40. Not merely architectural, but symbolic of purity, order, and restored worship.

The River of Life – Flowing from the altar, this supernatural river heals all it touches, transforming barren lands into fruitful places. Echoes appear in Revelation 22.

Twelve Tribes of Israel – The historic divisions of the people of Israel, restored and given land in Ezekiel's closing vision, signifying unity and fulfilled promise.

Bibliography & References
Biblical Sources

- The Holy Bible, King James Version (KJV)
- The Hebrew Bible (Tanakh) — Masoretic Text
- The Greek Septuagint (LXX)
- The New King James Version (NKJV)
- The ESV Study Bible, Crossway
- The NET Bible with Full Notes

Biblical Commentaries & Dictionaries

- Matthew Henry's Complete Commentary on the Whole Bible
- The Expositor's Bible Commentary, Frank E. Gaebelein (Gen. Editor)
- The New International Dictionary of Old Testament Theology and Exegesis
- The Zondervan Pictorial Encyclopedia of the Bible
- Vine's Complete Expository Dictionary of Old and New Testament Words
- The IVP Bible Background Commentary: Old Testament – John H. Walton et al.

Historical and Theological Works

- The Prophets, Vol. II – Abraham Joshua Heschel
- The Temple: Its Ministry and Services – Alfred Edersheim
- A Biblical Theology of the Old Testament – Roy B. Zuck
- Theology of the Old Testament – Walter Brueggemann
- The Message of Ezekiel – Christopher J.H. Wright
- The Glory of the Lord – Joseph D. Hall
- Holy Fire – R.T. Kendall

Academic & Supplementary Sources

- Journal for the Study of the Old Testament (JSOT)
- Tyndale Bulletin
- Bibliotheca Sacra – Dallas Theological Seminary
- Biblical Archaeology Review
- Ancient Near Eastern Texts Relating to the Old Testament – James B. Pritchard

Jewish Sources & Historical Insights

- The Mishnah – Trans. Herbert Danby
- The Babylonian Talmud (select commentary excerpts)
- Midrash Rabbah: Exodus and Leviticus
- Jewish Study Bible – Oxford University Press
- Ezekiel in Rabbinic Literature – Moshe Halbertal

About the Author

Damiano B. Centola is a visionary theologian, poetic thinker, and prophetic voice for this generation. With a background in Scripture, sacred art, and divine revelation, Centola has authored over two dozen Spirit-filled works that bridge ancient truth with modern hunger. From the Psalms to sacred geometry, from the cries of the prophets to the patterns of the tabernacle, his books call readers to return to the heart of God, to holiness, and to intimacy with the King.

He has ministered across cultures and continents, awakening hearts to the Living Word. Known for his reverence, clarity, and uncompromising pursuit of biblical truth, he writes not only with ink but with fire.

This is his 25th published book.

But to him, it's always the next surrender.

Dedication

To the Watchmen—Those who cry through the night

Not for judgment, but for glory.

To those who've stood when others ran,

Who've wept for a wandering people,

Who've fasted in silence,

Who've kept oil in their lamps.

To those who watch the east gate,

And wait for the return of the glory.

This book is for you.

May you rise.

With love, reverence, and eternal thanks,

Damiano B. Centola

Acknowledgments

To the Lord God Almighty—who opens heavens and gives visions to clay.

To my beloved wife, Feebe—my greatest earthly gift and the one who has walked beside me in every valley and mountain of the Spirit. You are the river beside the altar of my life.

To my parents, especially my father—the seer and spiritual well from whom I drink deeply.

To those who've carried scrolls, prayed through the night, and believed in what was unseen: your intercession gave birth to this.

To my readers around the world: You have made this journey sacred.

To every Ezekiel, every watcher, every heart that has longed for the glory to return—thank you. The fire has not gone out.

Note on Proportions and Diagrams

The proportions and diagrams presented in this book are intended to illustrate symbolic, theological, and historical insights drawn from Scripture, art, and sacred geometry. While grounded in anatomical and mathematical research, they represent interpretive models rather than clinical or universally precise measurements of the human body. Their purpose is not to claim absolute scientific accuracy but to reveal the patterns by which artists, architects, and theologians have discerned divine order in creation.

www.ingramcontent.com/pod-product-compliance
Lightning Source LLC
Chambersburg PA
CBHW051316120626
46547CB00015B/2257